To

HELEN

Bob W. Brown

4/10/76

How Can We Get Lily Rose To Settle Down?

How Can We Get Lily Rose To Settle Down?

The Thoughts, Tears, Prayers, Frustrations, and Victories of a People-Hearted Pastor

Bob W. Brown

impact
books

Library of Congress Catalog Card Number: 75-4160

ISBN 0-914850-28-8

MO528

To Helen
Jeff and Amy
Who Have Shared My Time With
So Many People,
And Who Have Loved Me.

Contents

No One Talked About People

The Ordaining Council solemnly laid hands on my head to "set me apart for the Gospel Ministry". There was a procession of ninety-seven ordained preachers and deacons at that service. The date was January 9, 1949. I was eighteen years old.

The "laying on hands" ceremony had been preceded by a two hour service. I had been sung to, preached to, charged, and challenged. There were six different veteran pastors on the program. They had talked about the joy of preaching, they had carefully examined me about doctrine, they had discussed church policy. They gave me a Bible.

No one talked about people.

As I knelt by the altar of my home church I felt surging and confusing emotions. I'm not sure how "spiritual" those feelings were. I felt some satisfaction and confidence. Many aspects of the pastoral ministry were attractive to me in 1949 and they still are. The "preaching" part of the ministry was exciting in 1949 and it still is. Kneeling there I felt that this was right for me. There wasn't a lot of anxiety, or fear, or awe. I thought I could be an effective preacher and pastor. I was thinking about me.

I didn't think much about people.

The church will bring you back to reality. The church is people. All kinds of people with all kinds of needs, all kinds of pain, all kinds of anger, all kinds of virtue, all kinds of love. They gather to worship with their diversity. They come to meetings with their variety of purposes. They call the Pastor in the night with their different problems. They refuse conformity. They resist programming. They will not, they cannot, be put into identified categories.

I learned to think about people.

It has been said that pastors handle the sacred. That pastors live in holy isolation. That pastors enjoy some mysterious relationship with God that separates them from the very human hurts and temptations of their parishoners. That they live in some kind of insulated ark of holiness and spiritual magic. No one who is a conscientious pastor escapes the ecstasy and the agony of humanity. There is no ark that fences in the pastor.

There are people all around the church.

The sensitive pastor wades into the human fray. He learns to weep. Long nights of tears. He learns to expect surprises, both good and unpleasant. He admits failure, despair, and futility. He knows anger and retribution. He is repulsed by the ugly and bizzare. He finds extreme kindness, gentleness, and generosity in unlikely places. Laughter and good humor spring up in desert places. And his ministry and his feelings involve people.

God doesn't zap out mature, contented, healthy people with assembly line precision. God doesn't perform magic tricks to alleviate human hurt and frustration. Answers are not always apparent. There is no "God machine" or "Church machine" with mysterious formulas and blueprints. The pastor and the church cannot push another human into a telephone booth, say "Shazam" and produce a Christian superman.

Lily Rose is about people. People in a city of 200,000 individuals. People in a three thousand member church. People who have touched my life during the past twenty-five years of pastoral ministry. People who are involved in my own intimate circle of family and friends. People who have responded to our effective television and radio programs. People I have talked to in hospital meetings, in stores, at ball games, on the phone, at funeral homes, in high schools, and on crowded streets. People who, for one reason or another, want to talk to a preacher. *Lily Rose* is about those people and the way one Pastor feels about those people. And the way that Pastor feels about himself.

Someplace in this book there is someone, some feeling, that you can identify with.

Preface

Writing a book is a risky business. Writing is different than speaking. There is a finality to writing. Pilate was right, "What I have written, I have written". Writing must have a purpose.

This book is obvious. The church is for everyone or it is for no one. No one is left out. Most of us would say that, but not many of us have practiced it.

I have watched the Trinity Baptist Church in Lexington, Kentucky practice that kind of open ministry. We have black and white people. Wealthy and poor people. University people and retarded people. Young and old. Hippies and squares. Blind people and politicians. Mountain people, Yankees, and foreign born.

Thanks to the church people who encourage me and our staff in a people ministry. Thanks to my family. And to my secretary June Picklesimer.

And to our Lord Jesus who loves everyone, including Lily Rose.

Bob W. Brown
Lexington, Kentucky 1975

houghts

Disraeli said "Experience is the child of thought"
The Mountain Man said
"I'm pondering it."

My Dad used to say "I'll think about it"
Erring thoughts. Wandering thoughts. .
"Think it through."

Paul said "When I was a child
I thought as a child —
But the man
Put away childish things."

Restless, confusing, tumbling thoughts.
Organized, ordered, structured
Thoughts.

Pleasant thoughts. Painful thoughts. Idle thoughts.
"As a man thinks in his heart
So is he."

What's Wrong With Being Nice?

There is this lady in my town. She is a doctor's wife, mother of several children, and active in civic, religious, and social groups. She usually shows up at community events and gives vocal support to worthwhile causes.

She's an attractive gal. Looks good. She also is an outgoing, warm and friendly person. She flatters people. Always seems to be interested in other people. Says nice things to and about people. Is never sarcastic or cynical. Doesn't seem to be up tight or on edge about people or things. I guess she is mushy. Too polite. Too flattering.

At least some people say she is just "too much" and she does come on strong. But I like her. My wife likes her. My kids like her. A lot of people like her. There are always people who criticize her by saying that she is "just too good to be true."

I've been thinking about that.

Wonder why we're so persistently suspicious of people who try to be nice? We all become guarded and afraid of these nice people. We're leary of someone who compliments us, or flatters us, or thanks us. We want recognition. We want to be noticed and to be listened to. We want to be appreciated. We want people to treat us kindly.

I think we want to earn recognition. We think that kindness should be earned or deserved. We are just uncomfortable with people who practice kindness. When someone goes out of their way to treat us with respect and when they compliment us without being motivated by any self gain, we become suspicious. We think that courtesy and kindness should be mutually productive.

And tonight I can't think of one thing that is wrong with being nice to other people. Not one thing!

What Is Man?

The Governor said that the tornadoes tonight had produced the most tragic disaster in the history of our state. Nearly one hundred people are dead. Hundreds are injured. People are missing, some presumed to be buried under rubble. Some were blown into the rivers. People are homeless, hungry and water is dangerously polluted. No one will ever know the amount of property damage.

Schools are morgues. Phone lines are out of order and distressed relatives in distant places are trying desperately to find out if their loved ones are safe. Doctors and nurses are working to exhaustion. Sirens scream in the night. Emergency vehicles stab the darkness with eerie red and blue lights. Police stop traffic and drive through the streets with loudspeaker warnings urging people to seek shelter.

There is no electricity. A great city lies still without power. No traffic lights or neon signs.

No electric stoves, refrigerators, or hot plates.
The wind roars and clouds look like moving pillars
of smoke. People huddle in basements and wrap
frightened children in blankets. Some listen to
battery radios and light candles. Hail stones are
actually as big as golf balls.

And I'm thinking as I sit in the shelter with my
friends about our limitations as men. In spite of
all of our marvelous scientific and technical skills
and knowledge, we are little children before the
tornadoes. With our amazing ability to learn, to
think, to feel, and to express our feelings, we are
but children crouched in a shelter.

I remember that the Psalmist said "What is Man,
that thou art mindful of him"? I don't feel so
big tonight.

The People

We have just gone through another national
election. Every four years we go to the voting
booths to elect a President. The candidates and
their supporters spend a lot of money to get
elected. They spend a lot of energy campaigning.
They get tired and the people always say that
they're glad it's over. Someone wins and someone
loses but neither man is ever the same again.

Seems to me that the winner never makes things
as good as he promised and it is never as bad as

his opponent told us it would be. The candidates invariably promise too much.

We have been fortunate in this nation because the men we elect have basically been committed to our kind of government. If any of them wanted to become dictators, they have been restrained in some way. If any of them were mentally unstable, their insanity was controlled in some way. Some of them were probably outstanding men of character, intelligence, and talents. Many of them were very ordinary. Yet the nation survives. The system works. The world is better because of the nation.

I think we exaggerate the importance of the man in the White House. I think we have always done this. We are conditioned to believe that the first Tuesday in November of every year is the most crucial day in history. It's not!

It's the people. Merchants selling shoes and bacon. Farmers stripping tobacco. Nurses taking blood pressures. Truckers hauling oranges. Sheriffs collecting taxes. Football coaches inspiring kids. Bands playing music. Mothers mending torn knees. Secretaries typing letters. Tired fathers mowing grass. Machinists making bearings. Physicians removing tumors. Grandfathers fishing.

The people. All of these people who care for their families, read books, sing songs, help their neighbors, attend their church, obey the laws, vote and look forward to tomorrow.

Worrying

I've been thinking tonight about the man who says he is worried about his falling hair. He's anxious about becoming bald. Another man is afraid that he will have a heart attack. A young man who has constant anxiety about a heart attack is also on my mind. A little girl said to me after Sunday School that she didn't know why her fingernails grew so fast.

There are farmers and builders who get uptight about rain and wind. They talk about the weather with great urgency as if their conversation will change the weather.

People often talk to me about the past. They wish that they had not married at an early age. They say that their time in military service produced unpleasant changes in their character. They tell about bad investments and money lost. They wish that they had bought a certain house two decades ago. They made the wrong choice about business or vocation.

People recite the past tense circumstances of failure. How they got into a mess. How they mishandled the crisis. How they fell into a trap. How they took bad advice and made bad decisions.

I'm prone to this pattern of thought. I guess we all are. We worry about things that we **cannot** control or change, like rain, baldness, and **finger-nails**. We replay lost ball games. Second guess decisions of yesterday. We relive past failures and mistakes. We want to make the present a recovery of the past.

This bogs us down. Paralyzes us. Inhibits us. We spend too much time worrying about things that cannot be changed. This is part of our weakness. Our great need? To be delivered from the past!

Going Home Again

I've been preaching this week in the community where I was raised. Things change. The city has encroached and what were grain fields have become subdivisions. Old ball fields are occupied by stores and filling stations. Some of the big trees are gone. Winding roads have become four lane highways. Our old high school buildings have been turned into elementary schools.

People change, too. It's been more than twenty years since I've seen most of them. Girls that I dated are now grandmothers. A boy I used to play ball with is crippled. We're all about forty and there are changes. Lines in our brow. Gray hair. We walk with a slower step. Funny, but my friends seem to have aged.

People that were old when I left don't seem much older—just the ones my age. A lot of the old folks are gone. Most of them have died, but there are some of the older ones left. It's good to see them and to remember things that they would never remember. Impressions they made on me when I was a child. Anecdotes that are pleasant to recall. And I remember some things that aren't so pleasant.

I've changed, too. Maybe we are, as a child, all that we ever can be as a man. But I'm not sure about that. Sometimes I wonder how much of what I am today is a product of that little town, of those people of yesterday, and of all that is past. Have I really changed, or do the passing years merely refine or accent what we are.

Well, I'll just have to think about that. Today I am what I am. And the people back there are what they are. Time passes. Towns, streams, and ball fields change. We change, too. And that's life.

Anyway it was good to be back there for a few days. To see some people again, some for the last time I suppose. And to enjoy some remembering. To know that nothing can ever be like it was.

A Surprise

Over the years I have talked with the lady on the phone four or five times. She is always pleasant. Makes proper small talk prior to getting to the point. She is an editor for a magazine that I do some writing for. I've corresponded with her probably twenty times. The letters are always warm, encouraging and to the point. She is a good editor and works for a good magazine.

A few days ago I flew into her city to meet with her and another editor about a writing assignment. I was excited about the assignment, naturally, and I was curious to see the two editors. They were to meet me at the airport.

I had calculated what a big city woman editor would look like. I figured she would be handsome, not beautiful. Tall and self assured. Well dressed. She is working in a hard, competitive field, so she would have a kind of toughness that would show.

What a surprise! She was in a wheel chair! Bundled up and sort of sprawled all over the wheel chair. Her muscle system is diseased and her body looks like it was put together by a mad man with no blueprints. She looked fat, but really was quite small. I do not believe that she has any use of hands or legs. There was something strange, nearly grotesque about it. I know that I stared at her like we always do at the handicapped. I know that I looked foolish to her. For some reason we always are afraid, surprised, embarrassed and self conscious around the handicapped.

The moment passed. She has endured staring people all of her life. Her mind is alert and sharp. Her good humor and wit brightened the day. Her smile is twisted, but genuine. Her editorial skills and her self confidence are evident. After awhile, I really forgot the wheel chair, the body, and the impotent helpless arms and legs.

Now I'm home and I wanted to pray for her. But I keep thinking about the way I acted when I first saw her. I suspect she copes with the disease much better than she copes with people like me who stop and stare.

Parents

I still have this boy on my mind these several days after Christmas. He has a little boy's mind in an adult body. He is mentally retarded, one of more than 100,000 mentally retarded children in Kentucky this Christmas.

The boy lives in a home for retarded children in our city. There are more than one hundred people like him in the home. About half of them come to our church. The home has modern and adequate buildings. Most of the workers there are conscientious and capable. They are interested in the children.

The home has a good program of planned recreation. The children play sports and games. The staff has analyzed the children. They have files and records on all of the children. They try to feed them right. They provide clothing and shelter. After all the kids are retarded. What can they really expect?

Well they got excited about Christmas. And we were able to do something there that the institution couldn't do. Personal gifts. A party. Santa Claus. A trip to a mall. Our people were thoughtful and generous.

I've never seen children any time or any place as excited and delighted with Christmas gifts. I'll never forget the sheer joy and enthusiasm of those kids. They literally jumped up and down when they opened their gifts. It was unforgettable. I am so thankful that I was able to see their joy.

But back to the boy. He has parents. He had expected them to come and see him. Instead they sent him a card saying they would see him in June. He was happier with the card from his parents than with anything else.

And I remember again that no love takes the place of a parent's love.

A New Life?

The man will soon be fifty. He is tall, gaunt and has a worried countenance. After we talked I can understand his worry.

Seems that he had his own business in a Texas town. There was an Air Force base near by and he made a lot of money. He went to church, attended P.T.A., joined civic clubs and was on the school board. Then he got mad at the preacher and quit attending church. It's been all downhill since.

The Air Force moved out and his business lost money. He came to Kentucky and made two bad investments. He now owes more than twelve thousand dollars to some pressing creditors. He is living under an assumed name, hasn't paid or even filed federal income tax for four years, has some stomach trouble and just got out of the hospital. Now he owes some doctor and hospital bills.

He has decided that all of his problems pivot around the church and his relationship to God.

He says there is no way that he can pay his debts. No one knows where he is or even who he is. He wants to move to our city and start over again with a new name. Says that he will get a job and keep his finances straight. Says that he knows he must get in a church and he wants to come to our church.

He told me all of this in confidence. Even told me what his name really is, at least that's what he says. And he told me what he intended to do in our city and what name he plans to assume. He wants me to keep his confidence, keep his secret and help him make a new life.

Sounds so simple.

But there can be no new life when a man assumes a name, ignores his honest debt and lives a lie. I told him that, but I've got a hunch he'll be at church Sunday. And then what?

Reconciliation

Preachers cannot, should not try to run the program of the church without the involvement and leadership of the laymen. The church does not belong to the clergy. The clergy does not have all of the answers. The clergy does not have any corner on expertise and judgement.

There is more to the modern church, or the ancient church, than progress groups and "spiritual" meetings. There are bills to pay. Decisions to make. Human needs to consider. Priorities. All of this is affected by our plans, goals, and needs.

So, like all churches, we have meetings. Committee Groups. Sessions. Boards. Councils. Conferences. All of these meetings eventually produce decision action and church policy. Occasionally those meetings backfire and we end up in conflict. When the group backfires, I'm disappointed because these small working groups normally help the people understand one another better and understanding is basic to love.

Anyhow the meeting blew up tonight. It was my fault. The meeting began too late. The men were tired. Two of the men have some severe pressure at work right now. Another one is having trouble with a teen-age daughter. Two of them just don't like each other. They never have gotten along and probably never will. I should have calmed them down or insisted that we go home and try again later.

But I didn't interrupt. No one else tried to calm them down and they had a bad time. Argument. Acrimony. Anger. Some of them were pretty rough on the others. They gave me a few bruises too...and I bruised a few.

We shouldn't have had the meeting. But we did. Now the thing is to get together, find a new place to begin, and act with some attitude of forgiveness. Or what is reconciliation all about?

Too Much Tolerance?

I guess I'm just tired and irritable. We've called a T.V. repairman six times. He has come twice and the set still isn't fixed. And that disgusts me! Not that the T.V. is all that important but a man should do what he is paid to do.

I think of the times that a waitress doesn't bring what you order and expects a tip; and a builder cheats on the building; and the auto mechanic doesn't fix the car.

In fact, most of us expect warranties and guarantees with everything we buy because we assume that there will be breakdowns, malfunctions, and necessary repairs. We don't really expect to get what we pay for.

Of course nothing is perfect. The Lord has taught us to forgive and reconcile.

At the same time I wonder if it isn't possible to develop too much toleration for error. Do we excuse too many things in ourselves and in others? Have we become so tolerant of mistakes that perfection and completion are obsolete?

Perhaps we can be too demanding. Too rigid. Too exacting. Too precise.

But I have a feeling that we can be too liberal. Excuse too much. Lower our expectations...our goals. Then it becomes easy to settle for second best, easy to fail, easy to be average in things that demand excellence.

How much can I expect of my church? Or from my children? Or from myself? Or from God?

The Book talks about an Excellent Way.

An Unfriendly World

I was listening today to an old Negro woman pray. She is past ninety. Lives with her niece. She has been totally blind for more than seventy years. Totally blind!

In her prayer she asked God to bless her as she travels through "an unfriendly world." She used that "unfriendly world" phrase two or three times in her long prayer. I guess the Lord has heard her say that a lot of times.

Makes me wonder. I wonder what it would be like to be totally blind. No sunrises. No red roses. No green grass. No color T.V. at all! When you meet a stranger you don't know how tall they are, or how they look. A sightless existence must indeed be unfriendly.

She is the daughter of a slave. She knows the things her mother told her about slavery. People bought and sold. Families broken up. And once she told me how it was with her mother after slavery. Her mother came to town. Unprepared for freedom. Unprepared to make her own way. It was an unfriendly world for the child of a slave.

All of the harsh and crude prejudice of the whites was pointed toward her because she was black. The back of the bus in schools, jobs, and rest rooms. Being black in a white dominated world would surely make "unfriendly" an apt description.

She's known it all. Poverty. Slavery. Prejudice. Illness. Blindness. Loneliness. Pain. I guess it has been unfriendly.

But somehow I don't really feel sorry for her. In many ways I envy her. She knows how to cope. She isn't angry, or tense, or filled with self pity. She is at peace with herself. Other people don't bug her. She enjoys her church, prayer, music, preaching, and her friends. She laughs a lot.

I guess she accepts an "unfriendly world." Maybe we all need to accept some things.

Giving Away Money

I had an interesting experience today. A wealthy man in our city gave away $200,000 to worthy charitable organizations. He had announced a month ago that he was going to do this and had invited people to write in their requests. These letters were screened by a committee of his associates and the need was determined.

They had a dinner and all of the recipients were invited. At least someone representing each of the organizations was invited.

This was an unusual kind of affair. There was really a pleasant atmosphere in the room. Although the people didn't know each other there was a relaxed mood and people seemed comfortable. I guess nothing can eliminate tension easier than giving.

I paid some attention to the man who was giving away the money. Like most wealthy men he is controversial in our city. He inspires mixed feelings. Some people are indebted to him, some fear him, some are suspicious of him. There is a great deal of devotion and there is some hostility around the man. I can't and don't pass any judgement beyond my personal experience and he has always been generous and considerate to me.

He obviously was enjoying this occasion. He seemed happy to be giving away a lot of money. When people tried to thank him or be sentimental in their thanks, he seemed embarrassed. I had the feeling that being thanked and appreciated wasn't very important to the man.

It was a good day for the wealthy man. He enjoyed it. He made giving away money seem like fun. He looked happy, peaceful, and pleased.

You know, maybe it is more blessed to give than to receive.

A Cry For Vengeance

We had a shocking, horrible thing happen in our town. Two men escaped from jail and went on a rampage. They murdered a minister and his two children. They murdered three more people in a motel. They were finally arrested.

There isn't much explanation to this kind of thing. People all over town are talking about it. They wonder. Some of them are angry with the jailer. Some are angry with the system. Both of these criminals were accused of serious crimes prior to their escape and both have broken jail before. Some of the people are asking why God allows such tragedy.

The people are afraid and perplexed. Sure, they know that every day children die of cancer, teenagers die in auto wrecks, young adults die of heart attacks. They realize that every day men die in armed robberies, in war and revolutions, and that some place in the world people are starving. But that doesn't upset us as much as murder— especially murder in our home town — especially murder of a prominent family.

I'm dismayed at the outrage of some of these people who are crying for the execution of these criminals. They are circulating petitions demanding the death penalty. They go to the funeral home and talk about the electric chair as they stand beside the caskets. They say that the electric chair will stop this kind of violence.

But it won't. We do not overcome violence by using violence. "An eye for an eye" will not change the world. We do not change people by killing them. Execution is not the way to right a wrong.

I'm convinced that those two murderers cannot

live in society. They are threats to life. But my problem is the unbridled attitude of revenge that I hear. It is discouraging. I can understand the grief, the shock, the fear, even the anger. But I'm afraid of the desire for vengence. I guess God has been hearing that for a long time.

A Card

At one time this man was an important leader in our church. The people elected him to several high offices in the church structure and he was considered to be one of our top men. He wasn't so popular but he was very pious. Usually in the church people attempt to reward the very religious by giving them responsibility and honor.

Well, he quit attending church. He did not quit dramatically. He just drifted out of church life. It's been a long, long time since he has attended any services of the church and he has long since been replaced in his elected offices. In fact, a lot of our people have probably forgotten him.

At least they had forgotten him for awhile. Then he started telling people that he had fooled the church. He says that he never gave his money, never more than one dollar per week, but the church elected him to direct the financial program. He says that the only time he ever prayed was when he prayed at church. He says that he never read the Bible from one Sunday until the next but could pass as a Bible expert. He has said a lot of other things about how he fooled the church people. He says the people are pretty stupid.

Three days before Christmas I saw him in the Post Office mailing Christmas cards.

What in this world could Christmas mean to him? He is a bore. A hypocrite. Christmas is for children. For giving. For generous, loving people. Christmas has an awe, a mystery, a reverence. Christmas is for believers. Believers who reach for a star... a manger...a child in Bethlehem. Christmas seems to preclude the cynic, the hypocrite, the bore.

But maybe I'm wrong. Maybe Christmas is a time, the only time, for a fellow like this to reach out to someone else. Maybe Christmas is also for the selfish and the arrogrant. Maybe the mystery of Christmas is wrapped up in touching a man like this.

He sent me a card. I guess he wanted to.

Laughing At Myself

The other day I walked up on some kids who attend our church. They were playing church and one little boy was imitating me. They didn't see me so they continued their game with enthusiasm. The little guy who was imitating me was quite an actor...perhaps entertainer is a better word. The other children, those in the "pews", were delighted with his performance.

It took the starch out of my collar! Made me realize that those kids don't take me nearly as seriously as I thought they did. And, of course, they don't take me as seriously as I see myself.

I laughed with them as they laughed at me.

It made me realize that life must be punctuated with some laughter. Religion must not always be grim and sober. We are all inclined to make worship and preaching, prayer and witness so very somber and serious. Irrepressible children know better. They know that God is not so frightening and awesome...that he can hear laughter easier than chants. He can see smiles as quickly as tears.

This little children's church charade helped me see myself better, too. A lot of things that I do and say are humorous. Not that I intend to be a clown, but like all adults I assume a posture of perfection. Kids see through it. They realize that we all say some ridiculous things. Our ego makes our antics pretty funny to a child.

I think of all the things that I've done that are silly. The unkept promises. The failures. The pompous pronouncements. The plans that never work out. The false conclusions I draw. The incorrect motives.

Sometimes God must be amused, too, at people like me. Well, at least the kids laughed. And I laughed too. These days a laugh is worth a whole lot. Even laughing at one's self.

Peacemaker

The firemen in our city are out on strike. It's an unpleasant feeling. Over the years you learn to expect them to be on the job. Occasionally in the night you hear the sirens. You know they are answering a call and you go back to sleep. They are competent men and there is some assurance in knowing that they are on duty.

When our church burst into roaring, frightening flames a few years ago, they answered the call. They didn't put out the church fire but they kept the fire from burning my house.

Now the Fire Department of more than four-hundred men has been reduced to about fifty to sixty men. It is an uncomfortable and potentially tragic situation.

They want union organized collective bargaining. The City Council is not willing to deal with public employees in that setting. They are at an impasse. It is unfortunate.

I understand the position taken by the Council and by the fire fighters. A lot of people feel strongly in both directions. There is a growing sense of frustration, anger, and hostility. Pickets. Slogans. Gossip. Politics. Fear. Confusion. Rigid positions...Inflexible attitudes.

We're supposed to be ministers of reconciliation. That sounds so good and so simple until we try to reconcile people who are emotional, unyielding and inflexible. We're supposed to be peacemakers. That sounds so simple until we try to bring peace when some people prefer confrontation and conflict.

So I've tried to be a buffer in this mess and it didn't go too well. But I think I'll try again. The Lord will have to help.

The Sixth Grade

The boy's Daddy drinks too much. He is abusive and loud when he drinks. He curses the little boy's mother, curses and beats the little boy and vomits all over the house. He can't keep a job and they are very poor. The house is delapidated and the little boy's clothes are worn out. Food stamps usually help them have enough to eat.

The little girl's grandmother is dying. She has been in and out of the hospital several times. Now she is back home. The grandmother loves the little girl very much and has always been tender and kind to the little girl. The little girl hears the grandmother groan in pain. She has watched the grandmother waste away. The little girl is hurt and perplexed. She grieves as she watches her grandmother die. Little girls do not understand death.

The little boy lives in a $100,000 house. It is something to see! There is a live-in maid. Big automobiles. Swimming pool and tennis courts. The little boy's father is well known in the city and the mother is a beautiful lady. They attend the right meetings, go to the proper dinners, travel extensively, join the right clubs. They are "leaders" in the city — but they never have any time for the little boy. They are not interested in his discoveries, his goals, his frustrations or his pain. They expect the maid to rear the little boy.

And there is the girl whose parents just divorced, and the black child who has felt prejudice, and the little boy with the hospitalized mother, and the boy whose sister is a hyperactive retarded child. There is the boy who feels neglected and the boy who loves music. There is the girl who has been stealing chewing gum and the boy who has a stomach ache.

All of these children and others are in the sixth grade class of the Sunday School. And some volunteer teachers who are tired and who also have personal problems will try to love these children and teach them the Bible. That's what Sunday School is all about.

The Old Church

The other day a couple of friends and I spent about two hours in an old church building. It was a disturbing experience.

At the present time the church has about fifty people who attend the services. Fifty years ago there were consistently more than two thousand people who attended and supported the church. About sixty years ago they built this particular building.

The sanctuary will seat more than two thousand people. Now about fifty rattle around in that splendid room. The stained glass windows were handmade in Southern Europe and shipped here before World War I. Craftsmen came on the boat to install the windows. One of them, an old man, died here and was buried here.

A great pipe organ sits idle and mute; there is no one to play it. Dust and cobwebs cover the pews in three balconies; they never use the balconies. In one large Sunday School room I found 1947 Sunday School books. They haven't used the room since '47.

I feel deeply about this. I think of the enormous waste. This magnificent building that is not being used at all. I think of the lost heritage. A building like that was built to stand for a century and it was built to be used. Those people who built it a half century ago made a sacrificial investment in the future. Someone has lost their investment. Someone lost their vision, their faith, or their willingness to sacrifice.

I realize tonight as never before that a church can die. That every generation must evangelize. Every generation must build its own churches and institutions. And that is a sobering thought!

Magic At Christmas

Some of the Christmas magic was tainted today. My little girl asked me some serious questions about Santa Claus. She can't believe in the **reindeer** and sleigh anymore. Or an old elf with twinkling eyes and a little round belly. She doesn't see how anyone, even Santa Claus, can get all over town in one night.

She isn't ready to discard it all. She's a little unsure and afraid that it might be true...and even more afraid that it's not true.

I remember that particular crisis in my own childhood. If it is all a myth, then it is a story of love and generosity carried out by parents. Parents who are so lavish in their love that they feel more comfortable using Santa as a pseudonym. ·

I figured that out. Santa was another name for Mother and Dad. In some ways it is easier for Mother and Dad to use that name.

When I put away childish things or things like Santas, buckeyes, ball gloves, fishing worms, and pocket knives, I learned as a man that children need Santas.

And more important, men need to be Santas.

So it has never seemed to be a myth, or deceitful, or play acting, or dishonest, or dreaming. It has all been part of our love in that wonderland of magic and hope between parents and child.

As she grows older, some of this will fade again.

Fade into something else...a more mature understanding of love and giving.

Then someday she will have a child of her own. The mystery of Santa will be reborn. Hope I'm around to see it. It's good.

The Sub — The Team

Like most of the people who live in my town, I enjoy basketball. The University has produced a parade of All American players. The coach has won more games than any coach in history. Every game is sold out and people stand in line for hours and hours to get standing room tickets. A lot of people call our city the basketball capital of the world. The good players become heroes...to adults as well as to children.

Anyhow, tonight I was watching one of those exciting ball games. The coliseum was packed to the rafters with a screaming crowd. The game was tied more than a dozen times. It was a championship game. The team was passing and shooting with remarkable grace and precision. Two or three of the more publicized players were having a great night. I was thinking that those stars would be in the headlines tomorrow. Their fame would grow. They already are among the best known people in the state.

Down on the bench sat another young man.

He wasn't in the game. He probably won't get in the game unless we are far ahead or far behind. He isn't famous. No headlines. No instant recognition. No autographs. He hasn't played in many games and won't play in many.

It is lonely and frustrating to be the last sub on the bench.

I suppose his primary role and major contribution is in the daily practice sessions. The stars scrimmage against him every day. They sharpen their skills at his expense. They build their reputations against his persistent pressure. He will never be a hero.

Suddenly the game is over. We have won again. The sub that I've been thinking about rushes out to congratulate and embrace the stars. He isn't frustrated, angry, pouting. He is, after all, part of the team. I think we need that spirit in our church.

Matchmaker

The man called the office and asked my secretary if I would stop by and visit him in the hospital. I didn't recognize his name, but I stopped at his hospital room.

When I went into his room he interrupted my introduction by saying he already recognized me. Said he watched me on television and needed my help. Said he "figured that a preacher could help him if anyone could".

42

The man asked me if there was anyone in my church that wanted to get married. He had decided during his stay in the hospital that he needed to have a wife. Well this kind of perplexed me. Don't often get that kind of request.

The man is serious. He was as serious about this as a man could be. He is past seventy-five. He said that his health was good. The main reason he was in the hospital was for a check up and he had decided that loneliness was getting him down. He calculates that he will probably live about five years. He would like to marry a woman who is sixty. By the time she is sixty-five he will probably be "dead and gone".

He owns some property and will leave her the property in his will if she will live with him for at least five years. He said that he has always done his own cooking and cleaning and she won't have to do that. He will expect her to talk to him, go to town with him and, he said slyly, "she will have to sleep with me".

The old man spoke precisely and with some enthusiasm. He obviously is excited about the idea. It represents quite a decision for him to make. He also speaks with some finality, apparently believing that if he makes that decision then the wedding will follow.

Ah, the pain of loneliness...and the delusion of loneliness.

But I'm thinking, maybe the old man isn't as strange or eccentric as he originally sounded. I don't have any ideas, but I just might think of a lonely old lady.

Conversion

The man was in an accident and has had both legs amputated. He has made a reasonable physical adjustment and his attitude is great. He was telling me that Ernest came by every time it snowed and cleaned the snow off his sidewalk.

Dad and Mother had water under their house after a severe rainstorm. Their pump wasn't working and the house was about to float. Ernest came by that night, fixed the pump, and stayed until after midnight to make sure that it was going to carry the water away.

Mrs. Childs is an eighty year old widow. She has enough money to get along. Ernest stopped by one day last fall with a chain saw to trim up some trees in her yard. He repaired a fence for her and adjusted the levels on her refrigerator.

When Carl's wife was dying in the hospital and she was in a coma for more than thirty days, Ernest took Carl's boys to a ball game...to Scouts...and more than once helped them with their homework. During Carl's wife's funeral, Ernest stayed with Carl's invalid mother.

I didn't know until today that Ernest takes the Adams shopping every Saturday morning. The Adams are a young blind couple in our city. It's hard for blind people to get to the store, so Ernest takes them.

Ernest is a good man. He is kind, thoughtful, and energetic. He doesn't brag about his good works. He doesn't advertise. He doesn't ask for appreciation or thanks. I really don't know a lot about Ernest. He is quiet. At one time Ernest was an alcoholic. At one time Ernest had a wife and children of his own. At one time Ernest wasn't a Christian.

He was converted and now he is a Christian. He has never told me about it. He doesn't have to.

Father's Day

Americans have an assortment of special days and holidays. Most of them have a valid reason for their designation and all of them have commercial implications. We're just passing through "Father's Day." There is very little similarity between the celebration of Father's Day and my own feelings about being a father.

No event is more vivid in my memory than the nights my children were born. Time stood still and a permanent picture was impressed on my brain. I know what the doctor looked like, I remember the sound of his voice, the nurses. And, of course, the way that the babies looked.

But there was and is more to being a father than standing awed in a hospital looking at a baby.

I've had to punish them when I didn't want to. In fact I hate to correct them, much less spank them. But I've spanked them, denied them, criticized them, disciplined them. And that's part of being a father.

They have cost money. They force you to change your schedules. They inconvenience you. They can irritate you. Children are never quite what you expect them to be. They can surprise you, and often the surprise is unpleasant. They change the way you live and dramatically change your purposes and goals in life. Nothing is ever the same again after you become a father.

Don't misunderstand. I'm not complaining. Quite the contrary. There is something indescribable, overwhelming, breath-taking about being a father. It's the greatest joy and most profound excitement that I know. The responsibility frightens me. The love involved is astonishing. I guess maybe I'm feeling just a little of how the Lord feels for His children — it feels good!

We Need Christmas

It's nearly Christmas. We need it this year. We need this holiday to interrupt our routine. We need the color of packages, tinsel, and tree lights. We need the excitement of children. We need trees, stars, candles, and songs. We need to give and receive gifts from loved ones.

I'm not sure what people mean by putting Christ in Christmas.

I think most of them mean a return to Bethlehem shepherds, angels, wise men, Mary, Joseph and the manager. They mean sermons and songs about His coming. And, I agree with this. We've lost some of the wise men's faith, the shepherd's adoration, Mary's wonder, and Joseph's patience. We've lost some of the miracle of Christmas. And a lot of us forget the Babe.

As I understand it, the Babe was sent to this planet because we needed Him. The first Christmas was a demonstration of God's love. We needed Him. And He came.

We need Christmas this year. I need Christmas.

For far too long we have walked in darkness — we need that great light. For far too long we have been unhappy and bored — we need abundant life. Too much of life has been crass and ugly — we need to see Someone who is lovely like a lily. We have too often been defeated and put down — we need to see a victorious life. Death is too real and unpleasant — we need to know eternal life.

We need Christmas.

We need to be reminded that other people care about us. We need to be remembered. We need a song to sing. We need a star to follow, a crib to kneel beside, a name to revere, a hope to cling to. We need an angelic word.

We need Christmas this year.

It's been a long time since Bethlehem. Come again. Do it again. We need Christmas.

Last Things

The other day my sister had a party for my Dad's 73rd birthday. Most of his relatives came. He enjoyed it and I guess everyone else did. It was unusual to have that many members of that family together at one time and at one place. At least it's unusual now, although in past generations it was an expected and normal thing.

Anyway, one of the younger guests remarked that this was probably the "last time" that they would all ever be together like that. The younger guest assumed that some of the older ones weren't long for this world.

But, I've been thinking.

There are "last times" all through life. Many are not as dramatic as death, but are just as final. Often just as painful.

I'm thinking of the last time that a boy climbs a tree. The last time a girl plays in her doll house. The last time your son sits on your lap. The last time a child goes off to school. The last time you throw a baseball in a game. The last time you go out with a gang of fellows. The last time you went to a certain house, or a certain job, or talked with a certain friend.

Life seems to be crowded with beginnings, and unfortunately, with bitter endings. I suppose nothing goes on forever. But we reach some endings, some finalities, with no warning, no preparation, and without even recognizing that it's over.

I'm not sure what we can do, or even what we should do about last things. Maybe we should just ignore these final things.

Maybe this is what the Bible means about "numbering our days." Maybe.

Like Father—Like Son

When Daddy died a couple of weeks ago, many people tried to be nice and said that I was a lot like him. They pointed out certain similarities.

He was a small man, I'm too large. He was quiet and I'm noisy. He was introspective, I'm an extrovert. When I was growing up I used to think that we were very, very different. And in many ways we were. In the most obvious ways we were different.

Now I have a teen-age son of my own and I see more clearly. We don't look alike either. Our external personalities are dissimilar. A lot of times my son, my Dad and I were together and I use to think we were a genuine study in contrasts.

But I know better. That is a superficial and fragile judgement. We are more like our parents than we ever know or dare to admit. Externals are precisely external. It's just like Jesus said, we are not what is on the outside, we are what is on the inside.

And so much of that inside me is what my parents put there. My sense of values. My moral judgement. My reasoning process. My sense of humor. My religious code. My character. All of that was planted and nurtured by my parents.

Whether I look like my Dad or not is really beside the point. He was a good man and he tried to teach me good things and that is the point. He wanted me to think right and feel right and that was always the way to be right.

Maybe the people at the funeral home are more correct than they realize. Maybe we all resemble our parents. And that's enough to shake us parents up tonight.

Too Big To Carry

We had been out quite late. Too late. My little girl had gone to sleep in the back seat of the car on the way home. I picked her up to carry her into the house. She draped over my arms, her head lolled back across my shoulder, her arms dropped across my chest. It was awkward. She is so long and heavy. She is nearly too big for me to carry.

She is only eight and too big to carry.

That thought bothers me. It hasn't been too long ago that she was so tiny. In fact she was nearly too little for me to carry. So small I was afraid that I would drop her, or squeeze her too tightly.

Then she was just right to carry. She grew as children must, and was still just right to carry.

Precious little girl. I guess I thought she would always be the right size to carry. That she would always fit into my lap and my arms. That somehow it would always be possible to hold her.

Daddys want to hold their children. Soothe their hurts, calm their fears, cuddle them, wipe their tears, tell them stories, read them books, laugh at their childish antics. Daddys want them to grow up normally and in good health, and daddys want them to always be the right size to carry.

But it's not that way, is it Lord? They grow up. Make their own mistakes. Choose their own friends. Play their own games. Laugh at their own jokes. Build their own worlds. Keep their own secrets. Some place along the line of growth they get too big to carry.

And I wouldn't really have it any other way. I want her to grow. To mature. But I also am kind of disappointed tonight that she is too big to carry.

Going Away and Coming Home

Some things worked out quite well and my family and I are getting ready to fly to Florida for a few days. I have to be in some meetings and we can work in some rest and relaxation as part of the trip.

51

I've been thinking and decided that this is something to pray about.

I'm really bone tired. There are too many visits, too much sickness, too many funerals, too much tension, too many drunks, too much divorce, too many meetings, too many kids in trouble, and too many unbroken hours. Fatigue is subtle. It is dangerous. So I'm thankful for a few days where the pace is different.

We live in a wonderfully small world. Children today can ride in a jet and see oceans, forests, and man-made marvels in a couple of hours. The world can be enlarged so quickly. Their vision and horizons changed by an airplane. I'm thankful for these unbelievable opportunities for travel for my kids. How different their world and mine.

I guess most of all I'm grateful for the anticipation and expectancy that we all feel. It wasn't a trip that we planned a long time. But we've talked about it long enough to look forward to it — to get excited. God, grant that we always have the ability to anticipate.

Finally, I'm glad that when a trip is planned, there is also a desire to come home. Maybe the best part of going away is coming home. Always when we go away, even for a few days, there is some anticipation about coming home. Back to a familiar drive, a familiar house, to pets, to the local paper, to trusted friends, to your church, and to people who love you and depend on you.

I'm thankful for this kind of going away and for the comfort of knowing there is something to come home to.

# Tears

Long Nights of desolation and despair
Embarrassing and hurting failure —
And I weep.

Death, graves, funerals and loss
Empty words and sadness —
And I weep.

No one really understands, nor can they
The journey is so lonely —
And I weep.

Anger and outrage overwhelm me
Screaming, striking are futile —
And I weep.

Sham and hypocrisy parade blatantly
Justice and mercy are gone —
And I weep.

But I'm Not Ashamed —
"Jesus wept."

Not Twenty

The girl wasn't yet twenty. She was so pale and drawn. Her skin was tight and fragile across her nose and cheek bones. Eyes were shadowed and circled...always vacant and staring into space.

She was in the hospital's intensive care unit.

Tubes and machines were keeping her alive. Solutions dripped into her arms. The expensive machine breathed, exhaled, and even sighed for her. Monitors recorded her irregular heart beat.

The doctors, there were two of them, stood by her bed. Nurses moved quickly to carry out the doctor's orders. Both doctors and nurses were weary. Their vigil had lasted for hours. One doctor was drinking some cold soup from a plastic cup.

Out in the waiting room her parents waited. They weren't any older than I am. This was their oldest child. They tried to talk to me. Small talk. Unfinished sentences. Broken thoughts. Sometimes pain and frustration is so deep that tears are absurd.

I sat with them.

The story that a nurse had told me was a long, sordid story. This girl, not quite twenty, was on drugs. Had been hospitalized and arrested for drug abuse. She had been hospitalized again with massive infection after an abortion. She was arrested and hospitalized again while drunk and incoherent.

Now the police ambulance had brought her in again...about two hours ago. Doctors aren't sure this time just what the problem is.

I was standing there when she died. No protests. No gasping. No crying. She just died. Not quite twenty.

God help us all.

Just Seven

I remember the night that the young couple came to the house. Her Dad was a preacher, too. His Dad was a big shot in town and a prominent laymen in a local church. They were both Seniors in High School. She was pregnant.

They were embarrassed. Frightened. Confused. They didn't want to tell their parents. They expected the worst kind of parental reaction — and they were right. The parents absolutely threw a fit. All four parents were angry. Loud. Unkind. Hurt. Embarrassed. I still remember the behaviour of the four parents. It was an ugly scene that night in my study.

The preacher father predicted that God would punish the kids.

They refused an abortion. They refused a home for unwed mothers. They insisted on marriage and, to everyone's surprise, they made it. He finished college and became an attorney. The first baby was followed by another.

They were good parents to those two little girls. The first-born is seven. It took nearly five years for the grandparents to accept the young couple. It took nearly five years for the grandparents to get over their embarrassment and hurt. It took nearly five years for the preacher and the big shot to become genuine granddaddies to the first-born girl.

Today the little girl was killed by a hit and run driver. I'm on my way to the funeral home. It's going to be rough down there.

The grandparents will be sure to place blame. The parents will be hurt so much. I want to help them all. They have been up tight for seven years.

A Lonely Boy

The children didn't know that I was around. They were in a small room in the church building. No adults were with them. There were four or five boys and girls sitting at a table talking. They had been playing and now they were resting. I guess they were six or seven years old.

They were talking about their parents. After all, that's what children often talk about. Their little world revolves around their parents. They make up imaginary characters, they talk about pets, school, and games. But most of all they talk about their family.

One little girl was saying that her Daddy read to her. He acted out stories, changed his voice and pretended to be a character in the story. He held her on his lap when he read to her. Another little girl said that her Daddy told her stories and played games with her.

A boy said that his Daddy had taken him fishing last Saturday. They didn't catch but one fish, but they sure had fun. This same boy said that his Dad kissed him good night every night.

I listened to these children and really felt good. After all, I have some kids of my own and I believe that at times they have bragged to other children about some good times we've had. And I was glad to know that some of our church children felt good about their Dads.

Then my eavesdropping was interrupted when I saw David, a little six year old boy, walk out of the room. David didn't see me. He went over into a corner and stood alone.

His Dad is in the penitentiary.

My heart goes out to all of the little boys and girls like David.

The Grandfather

The boy is in his second year at the University.
He was in court today for using and selling
narcotics. His hair is down over his shoulders,
trousers are dirty, sandals and no socks on a cold
fall morning. He was wearing an expensive, fringed
suede jacket. He has rings on four fingers of each
hand. He lives in an apartment that rents for more
than four hundred dollars a month and is driving
a brand new, expensive, foreign car.

He doesn't have a job.

I suppose they will convict him for selling
drugs and they will order some clinical confinement
to treat him as a user. I have the feeling that
society doesn't quite know how to cope with
drugs. Sure we have laws, research, trials, and
studies. But we still haven't decided how to cope.

The boy's grandfather sat by me during the
trial. He doesn't understand it all. He can't cope
either. He grew up on a farm and worked the
fields from daylight til sundown. Walked to
school and finished high school with effort.
He married his childhood sweetheart. Loved her
and lived with her for fifty-one years.

They sold their farm and moved to the city to
be near their two sons and their adored grandchildren. The old man gave the grandchildren
money along and had helped this boy get started
at the university. He hoped they wouldn't have to
work as hard as he had worked. He said that he
hoped they would enjoy things he had never had
time to enjoy.

Well, the boy hasn't worked like the old man worked. The boy hasn't worked at all. And the boy found some kicks that are strange and foreign to the Grandfather.

The old man doesn't understand. He sat quietly and tears ran down his cheeks when they prosecuted the boy. It wasn't at all what the old man had wanted. I guess God understands the old man; his children don't always turn out right either.

The Big Shot

I am praying for Vernon. This isn't the first time that I've prayed for him, but it's the first time that he has ever asked for prayer. Vernon has been in trouble for a long time. His friends knew it. His enemies knew it. Finally his family knew it. I suspect that Vernon was actually the last one to know it.

Vernon thinks he is a big shot. That's his expression, not mine. He was reared in an ordinary home. He has an average mind. He is an average looking man. He appears to be a normal, middle class white American insurance agent, but he has an abnormal drive to be a big shot.

He quit his insurance job and built a few houses a few years ago. He isn't a house builder by knowledge or experience. He began to pass himself off as an engineer, architect and designer. He built bigger buildings, and sold them all.

He bought a plane and took trips to Mexico and the Bahamas. He clubbed, partied, and got involved in politics. There were cute girls in his entourage.

Poor Vernon.

He really wants to be rich, and to live like the rich. He wants to influence people and to be a part of secret deals and manipulations. He wants to be admired and he wants to be feared.

But Vernon isn't really smart enough. His skills are limited. His knowledge is meagre. He can't produce and the tight money market has broken him. He has been in law suits and lost. He isn't clever enough to pull out of it.

Now he is broke. Humiliated. Defeated. Friendless. Some people are laughing at him. Worse for Vernon, most people feel sorry for him. Sympathy for the big shot.

I'll pray for him. But I'm not sure what can or what should be done for Vernon.

The Doctor And His Wife

This physician called me the other day. I met him in the hospital lounge. He is a handsome man ...a capable surgeon. People like him. I like him.

He told me that he had left his wife...moved out.
He said that she had driven him away talking about
religion all of the time.

According to the surgeon his wife was involved
in one of the charismatic groups that have grown
up all over America. Strong emphasis on the Holy
Spirit. They speak in tongues. Practice healing.
Study about the return of Jesus to earth. Most of
these people follow the same pattern. This used to
be associated with Pentecostal churches. Now the
groups include people from all of the "main line"
denominations.

Anyway, the surgeon's wife became obsessed
about healing. She kept telling him about the
healing miracles she had seen. A man had one short
leg and it was lengthened. People healed of cancer,
tuberculosis, ulcers, and backaches. She said people
were being healed of diseases they didn't even
know they had. They were being healed by laying
on hands, prayer, and faith. She decided that
medicine was a tool of the devil, that doctors
were not needed. She wanted her husband to give
up his profession and become a spiritual healer.

She also decided that he wasn't a Christian. Said
that he wasn't filled with the Holy Spirit.

He couldn't take it any longer and moved out.
But he feels badly. He loves her and he is
concerned. His mind tells him that she is
emotionally upset and needs some help. He thinks
that this is a phase that will turn and change, but
he also is a bit awed and apprehensive. He does
believe in God. He doesn't want to be against God.

The doctor isn't the first person to be mixed up

61

about the charismatic movement and he won't be the last. And people like me, who try to help some of these people, need the Lord's help. We really do!

A Love Affair

For a long, long time church meetings have been meeting places for people with multiple motives. Lonely people look forward to church meetings for they combat loneliness by being with friends. Aged people come to church meetings to break the routine of their life. Teen-agers have had "church dates" for years. There are people who use church meetings to promote their business, their politics, and their own image.

It's no secret, though rarely admitted, that some illicit love affairs begin and continue under the umbrella of church meetings. Some people who are looking for an extra-marital partner come to a church meeting to look. Churches do attract, and correctly so, people who are unhappy, frustrated, and weak. Consequently there have always been certain kinds of "affairs" going on in most churches. I guess some of these people are under the illusion that if there are religious overtones to their designs it will make them more compatible to conscience.

Anyway, Lord, we have one going on right now. I have watched it develop. I'm very reluctant to say anything. After all, it's presumptuous to accuse anyone. It's judgemental. It's suspicious. It's risky. It makes me uncomfortable. I don't want to create a scene.

But today the woman involved in this fairly obvious romance brought her daughter by my office. The daughter is thirteen. She has become rebellious. Won't go to school. Won't obey her parents. They say they don't know what to do with her.

The thirteen year old poured out her story. She knows her mother is meeting this man in the church. She says her mother is disgracing her father. Her mother is a hypocrite — a tramp, she says. She has no respect for her mother. She wants to hurt her mother.

Now I have to talk to the mother. Then I'll have to talk to the "Romeo" in the church. I'm not looking forward to any of it. I'm desperately in need of the Lord's help.

The Phone Call

I've about decided that there isn't much point in long phone conversations with people who won't identify themselves. They call to ask that I make a "surprise" visit on a relative. They call and pose hypothetical questions. They call to criticize or find fault. They call anonymously to pass on malicious gossip. They call to ask for help but do not want to tell who they are.

Usually there isn't much value in my listening to these conversations.

The man who just called didn't identify himself either. It's past 2:00 a.m. There was a lot of noise in the background. He said he was in a local bar. That's not unusual. A lot of 2:00 a.m. calls come out of bars. Noisy bars. Bar calls are usually from drunks.

This particular drunk admitted that he was drunk. Said he drank too much nearly every day. He's out of work, thirty-three years old and divorced. His wife married again and another man is rearing his two children. At this point he began crying. Drunks usually cry when they recite what their drinking has produced.

He said that he lives in a small room in a cheap hotel. Four walls. A portable television set with a distorted picture. He said there were two straight chairs and a roll-away bed in the room. He said that every morning when he woke up from his drunk that the room was like a jail cell. He said that every morning in that room he decided to quit drinking. Every night he got drunk again.

I asked him his name.

He told me that I knew him. His name was Lowell Walters. We were graduated from the seminary in the same class. He was an ordained preacher once.

He hung up the phone.

The Executioner

The United States Supreme Court has ruled that capital punishment is cruel and inhuman punishment. According to reports there are more than 600 people in America that have been sentenced to die. I guess people have some strange feelings because of that ruling.

I know a man who also has some strange feelings tonight. His name is Hudson. I first met him about fifteen years ago when he started attending our church. He was divorced. In his late forties. A very lonely, nervous, self-conscience man.

He had been the state executioner in a neighboring state. Seven different times he had thrown the switch for an electric chair. Seven different times he had seen men die in that chair. That was his job. He was paid to do it. I'm not sure if executioners are well paid or poorly paid, but it was a paid job. And it was a legal job, too. He was, in fact, carrying out the law. He was acting for the state and all the citizens of that state.

But it got to Hudson. It broke his spirit and his mind. He couldn't cope with it. He became too curious about the condemned people. He couldn't accept them as bodies to be burned. He began to see them as real people. He became curious about their families. He learned something about mothers, wives, sisters and even children.

Hudson quit after seven executions. He quit and he had nightmares. He quit, but he felt guilty and unclean. Hudson had legally served the state, but he felt that he had done an obscene, wicked, ugly thing. He thought that he had sinned.

Hudson told me that capital punishment not only was cruel for the men sentenced to die, but it was cruel to the executioner. I suppose Hudson is relieved now with the Supreme Court ruling — if he understands it. Hudson is in a mental hospital.

Suicide

This lad committed suicide this week. Today I conducted funeral services for him. He was eighteen. He was a big boy, more than six feet tall, more than two hundred pounds. He played football, worked out with weights, ran, swam, and played tennis. Until recently he attended our church regularly.

I've known him since he was a freckled faced, burr headed ten year old. He was an alert, friendly, happy little boy. I remember one time when he smashed his fingers in a car door and I took him to the hospital. He didn't whimper or complain. At that time he could endure pain. At that time life was laughter and movement.

His parents said that he changed about three weeks ago. He changed in a dramatic, frightening way. He was morose, depressed, listless and

66

preoccupied. At times he was irritable and **hypersensitive. He paced the floor and slept for** hours and hours. Lost his appetite and then ate voraciously. Kept his room dark and then would awaken in the night and sit up 'til dawn.

Finally he admitted to his parents that he was on drugs. He was frightened. He was horrified because of the changes the narcotics produced in his life. He was scared of his suppliers. He said that they threatened him. He was aware that his body and mind were deteriorating. He didn't see any way out. He didn't believe anyone could help, and he was afraid that if he sought help his pusher would do him harm.

He told his parents that he knew they were shocked and embarrassed. His girl friend wouldn't go out with him anymore. His coach wouldn't understand. His grandmother would be hurt.

The parents took him to a physician. He was referred to a drug clinic. He said he was afraid to go to the clinic.

So he went out and, like Judas Iscariot, hanged himself. Eighteen years old. Big, strong, and with so much of life in front. Now he is buried. He didn't see any way out.

And the pusher is alive and selling to someone else. I don't know, but something is sick in this kind of society.

Twenty Two Years

How long is twenty-two years? Long enough to go from high school to past forty. Long enough to see your children be born, marry, and give you grandchildren. Long enough to marry and divorce three times. Long enough to become an alcoholic.

Twenty-two years. That's how long Wallace says that he has been an alcoholic. He started drinking too much at nineteen. Now he is forty one. He started when Truman was President. We didn't know about Viet Nam, or Oswald or Martin Luther King, or moon flights and satellites.

Wallace doesn't know much about these things now. For twenty-two years he lived in the unconscious limbo of alcoholic stupor. He was unaware, uncaring, unfeeling.

He lost his home and wife. He lost jobs. He lost his self respect. He had no money and no job. He lived in flop houses and filth. Occasionally he'd spend a few nights in jail and dry out only to go back to the booze.

Finally he met a good woman. She loved him in spite of the filth and failure. She loved in spite of his poverty. She saw something in him that people hadn't seen for twenty-two years — something he hadn't seen himself. She married him. Went to A.A. with him. They came to church together. It was a new life for both of them.

After twenty-two years this fellow became a man.

I've known them for more than three years. He

has stayed off the bottle. Works every day. They bought a little house and seemed happy enough.

He came in today to tell me that he is leaving his wife and moving to Arkansas. Says he's going to remarry one of his former wives. The woman he's going to marry is an alcoholic. He says he is going to help her quit drinking.

It's hard to change after twenty two years.

The Doctor's Problem

They called me to the hospital last night. It was past midnight and the city was quiet. A cold rain was falling. I've made these trips often enough to have a feel of the night and emergencies. I've made these trips often enough to sense the city and to anticipate the hospital.

The emergency rooms always seem more white and bright after midnight. The nurses and aids always seem to be in a rush and they have a look of resignation. There is always noise in an emergency. Phone jangling. People talking. Patients complaining. Families murmuring. Everyone waiting anxiously for the doctor to arrive.

And as I drove along I was thinking about that doctor. Wonder how many times he has been called in the middle of the night to that emergency room? He will be there with the patient for a

69

couple of hours. He may have surgery the next day. Office hours. Interruptions. Some patients he can help, some that don't need help, and some no one can help. He works long days.

I was thinking about his wife and three children. His wife is an overbearing woman. She is unpleasant. Nags. Complains. Talks incessantly. She is materialistic and rude. He doesn't have much pleasure at home, I'm sure.

When he came into the emergency room he immediately went to work on our patient. He was rumpled. Unkept. Looked tired in his face and eyes. But he worked quickly and with competence. The nurses did his bidding. The patient was better. The family was reassured. Everything went great. The doctor was there.

He also had been drinking.

The last time I talked to him he had been drinking. And the time before that. He is drinking too much. It will affect his competence. He will make a mistake in judgement. He will cease to be an effective doctor. I'm sure that he thinks there are justifiable reasons. I'm sure that he thinks it won't affect his skills. But he is wrong.

May God help him...he has helped others.

Love

Harry said that he had always loved her. They grew up together in a small village. They walked to the little school together down by a singing brook. He had carried her books, defended her in childish skirmishes, and dreamed his dreams. In high school he had listened and watched as she flitted from one boy friend to another. Often at night he had stood under the stars and heard her out after her date had brought her home. They were friends. He loved her.

During their last year in high school she ran off with a boy from another town and got married. A baby was born. The boy wasn't ready for marriage or a baby. He mistreated her and finally ran away to California. No one has heard from him since. Harry took a pickup truck and moved her meager belongings back to her father's house. Harry loved her.

She wasn't ready to settle down. She used Harry in a thousand ways. Harry watched her baby when she went out. Harry loaned her money for clothes. Harry was always around when she needed help. Other people in the little town laughed at Harry. People had little respect for her and they thought Harry was a fool.

Another marriage and another baby broke Harry's heart, but it didn't really change anything. Now he took two children to the fair, to the movies, and for walks in the woods. He still gave her money. He still listened to her complaints and he still loved her.

71

Harry and I went to the jail last night to bail
her out. It was her first arrest, although it is
serious enough. Her legal husband is gone again.
Harry had her children when she was picked up.

I think she is a tramp. Harry loves her. God does, too!

Tension At The Funeral

I've always considered my work to be interesting.
Any pastor works with interesting people and he
is thrust into interesting situations. There is
variety in the ministers role and this variety takes
away boredom and routine. There is some drama to
the job. We are often with people in profound
experiences like birth, death, illness, baptism, and
marriage. Counseling usually has its share of emotion.

Last week a man was murdered. He was shot
four times by a business competitor. Front page
news story. Headlines on the television news. I
happened to know both men. The murdered man
attended our church. They called me, and there
was some drama to that.

They asked me to conduct the man's funeral.
Funerals are always tough. I've conducted
funerals two or three times before for someone
who has been murdered. I've had too many
funerals for young parents who have died
suddenly and violently. Usually they are killed in
automobile wrecks. There is a lot of tension at the

funeral of a young person who dies violently and suddenly.

There was some bad blood between the families at this funeral. Some of the relatives of the dead man were angry. Some of the relatives of the murderer were there, too. Both groups were sullen. Murmuring. Threatening. There were two detectives there. They were very visible. Their guns showed. I have the feeling that many of the people had guns.

Then, too, the man who died was a black man. I am a white preacher. The black mortician said that he never remembered a white preacher conducting a funeral for a black man. There was some conversation about that, too. I was perfectly aware of that interesting part of the service.

But you know when the widow and those four little children sat down by the casket of that young husband and father, I realized how unimportant all of the drama and tension were. How insignificant black or white is. I pray for that widow and those children. For their sake may God help us to eliminate violence and prejudice.

The Father

I suppose some people just try too hard to win approval, or at least to prove something to themselves. It's been a long time since World War II. Most of us have forgotten that during that war it was hard to be a German living in America, especially in a small town — a small town where Germans were unusual. And yet this is where Mr. Huffinger found himself in 1944-45.

He arrived in this small Kentucky town by a circuitous route that began in Germany in 1938 and led him through Europe, Canada, Ohio and eventually Kentucky. He had left parents and some brothers who were German soldiers behind. He saved a little money along the road. Married a German girl in Canada.

In 1944 he bought a small farm. He thought that he could gain the admiration of his American neighbors by making the little farm like the one he remembered in Germany. Even when the neighbors shunned him, he worked. When they insulted him, he worked. He made the farm look like a picture. It was a profitable farm for him and he accumulated some money.

When the war was over Mr. Huffinger expected people to change toward him and his family, but they didn't. Not that he really cared. Not that he understood. He consoled his lonely wife and two daughters by assuring them that hard work would eventually win respect. He was not lonely because his work was his companion.

The son was born after the Huffinger daughters were in their teens. The son idolized his father. He wanted to follow him to the barns, the fields, and the market. The boy was not lonely. He had the companionship of the farm and the father.

The father had no time for the boy. He always told him he could farm when he became older. The father said that the farm was a jealous master.

The boy told me all of this today. The boy is in jail in our city. I called the Father, but he said he was too busy to come.

Who Cares

The funeral is over. It was another one of those funeral calls prompted by our radio and television ministry. I did not know the deceased. I did not know anyone in his family. They have no church, no minister, no stated faith.

He wasn't old. His corpse didn't look old. He looked anxious, perhaps perplexed is the word, lying in the cheap coffin. Maybe he didn't understand death and apparently had never understood life.

He had moved away from here several years ago and had left a wife and four children. She married again and was very conscious of her behaviour, so she didn't really show much feeling. Her children are in their teens. They looked at the body of their father but they didn't know him, so they didn't know how to act either.

There were a couple of brothers. They are respectable middle class Americans. He wasn't respectable and they had not "been in touch" for more than a dozen years. The brothers wanted to care, probably did care, but it was all a bit embarrassing to them, so they busied themselves with taking care of the "arrangements".

And there were fifteen or twenty mourners. Some of them were old boozing buddies. Ragged clothes. Worn shoes. They were already saturated and numbed for the day. They were bleary and insensitive. They didn't respond.

Maybe I'm just being sentimental but his perplexed expression wasn't difficult to understand. He had lived nearly fifty years. Now a procession of people looked down on his dead face and no one really cared...at least no one was able to say they cared.

No wonder he was perplexed. To live and die and no one care. And I wonder if I cared, either.

The Mismatch

It is so obviously a mismatch. The man is slow, dull and a bore. He is one of the most self-centered men I have ever met. He drones on and on about his insignificant, drab, selfish existence. His conversation is at best innane. Most of the time it is intolerable. He explains in detail, without allowing an interruption, just how he told the filling station attendant to clean his windows. He relates endless monologues about something he heard at work. He is not interested in the children and is oblivious to their bids for attention.

She is about seven years younger than he. She married young, like so many kids do, so that she could escape a bad relationship with her parents.

She is an alert, attractive, interesting girl. She is vigorous and enthusiastic. She is excited about the tomorrows. She is warm and open. People enjoy her company and she enjoys people.

She despises her husband. He ignores her as if she were nonexistent.

I really can't see any way that these two people will ever be happy together. There is an inherent conflict in this marriage. I don't know of any common ground for them to meet on, no common tie to bind them, no common course to hold them together. Their marriage is a trap.

Except for the children.

And, that's the rub. The children need both parents. They love both parents. They love the self-centered father who ignores them. They love the restless, unhappy mother who screams at them. They find some security and some meaning by belonging to this family. So I tell the parents to stay together for the children.

And tonight my heart goes out to this miserable family.

Where Are They?

I've just come from the apartment where Carolyn lives. It's a nice apartment — expensive and luxurious. She has crowded it with furniture and momentos from her house. She sold the house and most of the furniture last week end.

She is a widow. Her husband died on November 13th at 6:00 p.m. Every time she refers to his death she recites the exact date and the precise moment. He had called her at 6:00 p.m. to say that he was leaving the office and was on his way home. He was an attorney and one of the most prominent men in our city. Everyone knew him. He created profound influence in politics, business, and the culture of our city. He was a key man.

She called to ask me to come by. They were not members of our church. I knew her husband personally and by reputation. I had never met her before. She is not quite fifty. A handsome woman, except for some pain and bitterness that shows in her eyes and can be heard in her voice. She is apprehensive and jumpy.

Seems that more than one hundred friends came by her house the night he died. There were more than eleven hundred people who signed the book at the funeral home. It was a huge funeral. The Pastor said the appropriate words. The friends were all there.

He had all of the business affairs in order.

A correct will. Plenty of insurance. She has considerable income and security. She also has a good religious background. She is anchored in the faith. Heaven. Eternal Life. She believes that the Lord called him home. I'm sure she is honest about this.

But she is lonely — horribly lonely. She has no children, no brothers or sisters, no parents or grandchildren, no jobs, no responsibilities, and no visitors. No one calls or comes by. Her eleven hundred mourning friends seem to have forgotten her. She is close to despair. When she talks about her eleven hundred friends she wonders, "Where are they?"

The Old Man And The Boy

Everyone talks about juvenile delinquency because it is a growing problem. There really aren't any easy or obvious answers. The Juvenile Judge here can, and does, require that some of these kids and their parents attend a citizenship school. This "school" meets once a week for seven consecutive weeks. The kids and their parents must attend.

Anyway, they asked me to speak at the school last night. I went into this room with about sixty "in trouble" kids and their parents. There were some familiar faces. I knew some of the kids from church and some of the parents by name or reputation. It might be good for more people to walk into a room like that and see just who is in trouble. They are not all poor. Not all black. Not all long hairs.

After the meeting was over and I had finished my talk, an older man and his son came up to me. The older man was terribly crippled — legs distorted — back deformed. He drooled when he talked and it was very hard to understand him. He had been drinking, at least he smelled strongly of drink. He wanted to know if I could drive them home.

The boy was tall, rather handsome, and very quiet. The old man growled and fussed at the boy and about the boy on the way to their very poorly kept apartment building. There is no mother. She had left the old man with the distorted body.

I let them out and the boy wandered up the street toward a gang of kids on the corner. The old man dragged himself toward the corner saloon. Neither one even considered going home. I guess there was no reason to go home. They went their own way. The boy is in trouble with the law. He will be again, I suppose.

Routine and Regimentation

It was pouring down rain when the phone rang. One of the sunday school teachers was in the church building getting her room ready for

Sunday. She and her husband discovered this man sitting outside my office door and they called me.

He had come to the church in a cab. He had spent more than sixteen years in military service. Things had gone reasonably well in that routine. His life was highly ordered and he could function in the regimen of a military structure. His problems came when he was on his own and was not restricted by military procedure.

His problems had compounded. He had been married three times. Two of the divorces came while he was in service and there weren't many scars. The last divorce had messed him up severely because he had married his brother's wife. She lived with him for nearly one year, then she divorced him and remarried his brother. By that time he was out of the service.

Three marriage failures were extended into civilian employment. He couldn't hold a civilian job. He had tried at least a dozen jobs and quit, or was fired, every time. Nothing was working.

Depressed and lonely he had admitted himself to a Veterans Hospital. He had stayed there as a mental patient for more than a year. He was not satisfied to be in the hospital because he was not really sick — physically or emotionally. But he was more comfortable in the hospital than on the "outside". He was now an out patient, and he was miserable.

So he came to the church on a rainy, gloomy Saturday night. A man who wants the security and routine of the military, or a hospital. Anything but freedom and responsibility. He wants to be told what to do. I guess that all of us have some of that in us.

My Mistake

I've made a mistake! It's not the first, won't be the last. It's not the most serious, not the most willful, not the most lasting mistake. But it is an error. Insensitivity. Sin.

Three or four times over the past four months Betty has asked me to talk to Paul, her husband. Just for the record, I don't really like Betty. She is a chronic complainer about the church. She picks at other people and gossips. She is an unpleasant, disagreeable woman. She doesn't have many friends, and like some people with her personality disabilities, she is always at the church. Every time the door is open, she is there.

Paul and I are friends. At least we get along well and make small talk. He doesn't attend church regularly, although occasionally he gets excited about something and is pretty active for awhile. I've always calculated that he quit coming to church because Betty bugged him so much and she embarrassed him.

Anyway, she has been telling me that Paul is cracking up. Mentally ill. She wanted me to suggest that he go to a psychiatrist. She wanted me to at least come by and see him and tell her what I thought about her diagnosis.

I kept putting it off. I don't like her and didn't trust her judgement. I didn't want to "spy" on Paul and try to decide if he was sick. So I didn't go.

Today he went completely berserk. Went around town on a buying spree and ordered more than $3000.00 worth of red carpet. Bought two red automobiles — both new. Stripped off all his clothes in a downtown men's store and kept yelling about red underwear.

I went with Betty to get him committed. Maybe I could have helped. At least I could have been interested. And I'm sorry. So very sorry.

Solitude

Mr. Kemper died tonight. He had been in the hospital for two or three weeks. He had been dying all of that time. He didn't have much pain. He didn't complain much. He didn't go into a coma until two days ago. I visited him nearly every day. It is always unpleasant and disturbing to watch a man die. Especially a good man, a kind man, like Mr. Kemper.

Mr. and Mrs. Kemper didn't have any children. They had been married for more than forty years. They had a good life together. They lived on a little farm at the edge of the city. They accumulated some money and they enjoyed traveling together. They stayed at home in the evenings. They planted things and watched them grow. They enjoyed their house and it always had the look of being lived in.

When Mr. Kemper died the hospital called me. I got out of bed and rushed to the hospital. They said that Mrs. Kemper was already gone. She was in the room with him when he died, left instructions to call the funeral home, and drove herself home.

I drove out to their house. A light snow was falling and it gave the night a subdued brightness. There was that strange quietness of snow, moonlight and the hush of 5:00 a.m.

There wasn't a light on in the house but the car was in the drive. I tapped on the door and Mrs. Kemper let me in. She wasn't crying.

She told me she just wanted to be alone for awhile. Yes, she would like for me to stay, but she wasn't ready to talk.

So I went into the den and sat. She sat in a big chair in the parlor. His big chair was next to hers. Empty. Forever empty. Occasionally I would hear her move, but it was extremely quiet. I guess that the next two hours were the quietest moments of my whole life.

As the sun began to rise she came into the den to talk to me about the funeral. The solitude was over. Now the business of life — and burial.

Sara Jane

Her name is Sara Jane. The youngest of eight children, but not really young. She is nearly forty. She is too tall and too raw-boned to be attractive. A school teacher. In fact she fits the stereotype for an old maid school teacher.

Sara Jane is shy — painfully shy. She has always lived at home with her parents. She attended college and stayed at home. Teaches in an elementary school within sight of her parent's house. Walks to and from school every day. She doesn't drive a car. Attends church occasionally and sits on the back row. Not many people in church know her.

Her mother was a strong-minded woman who completely dominated her father. She tried to dominate all of the other children, but one by one they left her tight fitting nest and married. They all moved away to places like Boston, San Francisco, and Miami. Two of the boys made a career of military service.

Sara Jane never left home, apparently made no attempt to leave home. Her mother had a heart attack and died in the kitchen. Within a week the old man was dead, too.

That was about a year ago.

Today Sara Jane came to see me. Seems that she had found a boy friend. A younger man. She met him at the school. He lives in a neighboring city. They have dated regularly for about three months. Sara Jane said that she didn't know that anyone could be as happy as she had been the past three months. She is really in love and she has never been loved before. In fact she has never dated before. She thinks they will get married.

I know the young man. He is already married and has two children. About two years ago I turned him up in another escapade of adultery. He is a rascal.

I feel so hurt for Sara Jane. I want to help her if I can.

Prayers

Some people compose prayers that sound good —
For the missionaries
For biscuits, bacon and beans
For the lost.

I have prayed at every kind of church gathering —
And meetings, conferences, groups.
It's religious.
It's O.K. with me.

In misery and fear I've prayed
for forgiveness,
for guidance,
for courage.

The more I pray the less I know about —
The more hesitant I become.
God is nearly too much!
We are not "buddies".

Occasionally I talk to Him comfortably —
Like Father to son.
He loves me.
He understands me.
He listens!

The Package Pastor

A lady called me on the phone and was quite upset with me. Said that she had been listening to me on television and that she didn't like it because I was trying to be funny. She said that people shouldn't try to be funny when the world was in such a mess. She said that preachers especially should be serious.

This call reminds me of the lady who told me that I wasn't dignified enough. She thought that a preacher should be easily identified in a crowd because of his dignity. This one thought that dignity was a Christian virtue and a ministerial requisite. Ministers should be called by a dignified title, dress in dignified clothes, and speak in a dignified tone as they talk about dignified subjects.

Well, Lord, I know that no one can be all things to all people.

But I've been thinking. The first lady is right. There is enough war, hatred, pain and death in our world. Every day I talk to someone who is hurting. Cancer. Heart disease. Age. Retardation. Blindness. Kids from broken homes. Poverty. Prejudice. Our world is always under the shadow of hurt. At the same time there seems to be some value in humor. A smile or laughter may not change anything that is wrong, but it does make some circumstances endurable.

I guess dignity is part of this dilemma too. No one wants to be a stuffed shirt. Aloof. Unapproachable. Withdrawn. Somehow these things are what people mean by dignity.

In either case people are trying to put preachers in a category. No humor but plenty of dignity. They attempt to wrap up, package and ribbon the preacher. Make him dignified and humorless, solemn and straight.

That won't do it as long as You have to use humans to be preachers. We have to be people, too.

I Wonder

As long as I can remember I've attended church. As a child my parents took me to church. My memories of being a little boy are built around a church, playing ball, and a good family. Looking back I realize just how much the church has dominated by life. Since I was a teen-ager, the church has dominated my life because that is where I work. I have always been a Pastor.

Maybe it's my age. Most men past forty begin to wonder about their job. I guess that men my age begin to wonder about most things. Maybe it's the tempestuous times we live in. Seems to me that every traditional value, every traditional institution, is fragile and shaking. I wonder if anything is like it was when I was a boy, when I was ordained.

Anyway, Father, I have these recurring doubts about the pastoral ministry. I can adjust to change in church life, in fact I welcome a lot of the change — even encourage the changes myself. There are a lot of rigid and useless things in the church that are stifling and wrong.

It's not change that bugs me. My doubts have
to do with people. Some of them are so immune to
love. They sit in church all of their life. They act
like they believe. They give a certain kind of
support to the church and to the gospel. They
make you think they are sincere. They act like
they are on the right side.

Then they get angry with one another. They
suddenly become vindictive and pouting. They
drop out of church. They find fault. They use the
church. They whack the pastor. Sure, I know that
church people are just people and I always say
that the church is for the weak, the sick, the
sinful. I don't think that I'm perfect and I don't
expect them to be.

But I can't help but wonder tonight if we
really accomplish much in improving human
behaviour. I wonder tonight if anyone is really
helped by my ministry. I guess You wonder, too.

For Christian Unity

I realize that Your Church has divided into
various groups and denominations. This worries a
lot of sincere people. They think that the
churches should all unite and do away with all of
the labels. They talk about and pray for a giant
church — a world church.

This doesn't really bother me. I believe that in
your economy we need different churches and

different kinds of churches. People have different tastes in worship and there are various churches to satisfy those tastes. People respond to different disciplines; they have different interpretations of life and different churches meet those needs.

I believe that if we abolished all of the differences between Baptists and Nazarenes, Catholics and Methodists, Pentecostals and Presbyterians that within a generation there would be the same variety of churches that we have today. Maybe they would have other titles, but they would have the same functions. People are different and churches just reflect those essential, and important differences.

Now having said that, Lord, I still pray for Christian unity. I'm ashamed and embarrassed when Christians of any label, or any denomination, put down other Christians. I'm embarrassed when churches hassle and quarrel. When they criticize and find fault with other churches. Surely we can acknowledge our differences without assuming some kind of superiority and arrogance.

I pray that we will love other Christians. Respect other beliefs. Honor other churches. Tolerate differences. I pray that we will allow, even encourage, people to be different. I pray that we will find a unity in our devotion to Jesus and find strength in respecting others — even those that we think are wrong.

For The Zealot

I'm not sure about this prayer, but I have to let out some of my feelings and You're the only One who can understand. Maybe some of my problem is defensive. Maybe I'm too judgemental. Maybe I'm missing something and maybe I'm wrong.

I've become extremely concerned about Lacy. Lacy is a college educated, self employed, reasonably successful realtor. He has been a member of our church for seven or eight years and has always been active and regular in attendance. The church has elected him to several offices and he has always filled those offices with grace. He prays in public, tithes his money, and invites people to church.

He became "revived" about fifteen months ago. Had a new experience with the Holy Spirit and has become more and more enthusiastic. Now, Lord, You know that any church needs some enthusiasm and any person is happier and more successful when they are enthusiastic. Sometimes his enthusiasm was hard for people to take. He turned off a lot of his friends, but I figured that they would come back to him.

Then his enthusiasm began a subtle process of change. He became more rigid and inflexible. He quit being enthusiastic and excited and became more overbearing and offensive. He didn't listen to anyone else. He wanted to argue Bible all of the time. He boasted constantly about his private Bible and prayer habits.

It was just a half-step from his rigid self righteousness to hyper-criticism of other people. He found fault with everyone. A lot of things he says about people are true. His attitude became cynical — hard — caustic. He hurts people and claims that You told him what to say. He assumes some special knowledge of right and wrong. He thinks he is right and everyone else is wrong.

Perhaps I'm too hard on Lacy. He makes me uncomfortable. He irritates and angers me. Maybe he is losing his mind. Maybe he has lost it. Maybe he is right and we're all wrong. Maybe he is a true Zealot. But is that good?

Divine Healing

Carl is about my age. He has a successful hardware store, three children and a good marriage Two years ago he was toppled with a severe heart attack and spent three weeks in the hospital. He was close to death for days. Carl is a religious man. I have no doubt that he is sincere in his faith.

He has decided that men live or die by faith, not by medicine. Consequently, he does not rest like heart patients should. He is overweight. Doesn't exercise. Lifts and goes up and down stairs. He deliberately defies the doctor's advice.

They put him back in the hospital. He was told to go back, but only consented when chest and arm pains were so acute that he had to go. He still says that the doctors are wrong and he is trusting You.

Joyce has a big tumor on her lower leg. It is ugly, uncomfortable and discolored. She's walking with a limp and is in pain. She has two children and a good husband. Her husband is absolutely frightened speechless because she won't go to the doctor. She claims that You are going to heal the tumor without medical help.

I've known Tim for several months. He is past twenty — extremely moody and self centered. He doesn't work or go to school, is suspicious of people, and sits in his room during the day and prowls at night. He believes that people are conspiring against him. He is obviously and dangerously mentally ill. I fear for him and his parents. At best he is wasted and unhappy. It is more likely that he will kill himself and someone else.

His parents say that medical care would be a lack of faith. They believe that you will "guide him in the way he should go and that his withdrawal is because he is under conviction."

There are some strange things happening today in Your Name, and it's not easy to cope with them.

Weakness

We're not much on self-control and self-discipline. Most of us are self-indulgent and we excuse a lot of things by saying "I really shouldn't, but I just can't help it." At this point I'm as weak and self-indulgent as the next person.

Some of us eat too much. We gain too much weight. It's bad, but we still overeat. Or we eat things that we shouldn't. Or we eat at bad times. We neglect exercise. Don't get enough sleep. Smoke too much. Drink too much. None of us really plan to get sick, or wear out, or abuse our body. But we do it, because we don't have self-control.

We have the same problems with our emotions. We are impatient and harsh with the people around us. We are unkind to our mates, quick tempered with our children, and irritable with our parents. We are cross and moody with our friends. We don't really intend to hurt people, but we don't have enough self control.

We do it with money. We spend money we don't have. We buy things we don't need. We waste our money and then we always feel financial pressure. It's not that we are poor, but we simply don't exercise self-control about our finances.

At times we get carried away in conversation. We tell big stories. We exaggerate and embellish. We gossip and lie. We do not plan to lie, but we talk too much and say things that aren't true because we don't have enough self-control.

We aren't very strong, Lord. We walk the wrong roads, make poor decisions, exercise faulty judgement, love the wrong people, waste our time, misuse our talents. We hurt others, impose on our bodies, mistreat our loved ones, and sin against You. We sure mess life up.

In spite of this weakness and self indulgence,
You love us. And I wonder why?

Ordinary Men

I just came home from a church convention.
Most of the people present were preachers and
preacher's wives. This is one of our big problems
in the institutional church. Most of the decision
making is done by the clergy. We have divided up
the ministry among the "professional" churchman
and the laymen. It's unfortunate and contrary to
your plan for the church.

When you're in this kind of meeting dominated
by the preachers, it puts some things in proper
perspective. For instance, most of these men are
held in some esteem in their own church or they
would not even have a church. There is some
mystique about the titles "Reverend" or "Pastor."
These men are present at certain sacred occasions
like birth, death, marriage. These kinds of occasions
enhance their reputation, and they invariably have
an aura of piety. Some of them cultivate this
impression. They try to be good — to speak
religious words with a religious tone. They try to
be properly indignant about sin, properly enthused
about religion, and properly self-disciplined. They
know how to pray out loud. They learn what people
expect, or at least what they think people expect.

But it's different at a convention of preachers.

Put them among other preachers, loose from their moorings and the facade of their parish, and there is a change. Oh, they don't behave in wicked, bizarre, uncouth ways. They are very conscious of their behavior.

They are more human among their peers. They reveal their boredom with endless conferences and boring sermons. They admit their insecurity and their doubts. It is apparent that most of them don't have any potential for greatness. They are not particularly smart or clever — not unusually gifted. It is not a great pool of intellect or pragmatism

More than anything else it is apparent that the ordained ministry is crowded with ordinary men. Good men, but just ordinary men. You have been able to do quite well with ordinary people. I'm glad, for there is nothing extraordinary about me. I'm glad that you pick and choose among the willing.

A Burr Hair Cut

I'm not really surprised because people joke about thin hair and bald heads. To the delight of barbers and hair dressers, humans always seem interested in hair. Now men have their hair styled, too, and as one who grew up in a less style conscious era it always surprises me to see a man in a beauty shop.

Men are growing beards, side burns, and chin whiskers like they did during the American Civil War. Men wear all kinds of fancy, expensive toupees and kids, boy kids, wear their hair so long you can't tell boys from girls.

My hair has been falling out by the handfull for more than twenty years, and my balding top doesn't bother me one way or the other. In fact, being bald certainly has advantages.

But lately I've let my hair grow long and my sideburns are a little unruly. People rib me about it in good humor, and I don't take it seriously.

Well, this evening a fellow came by the office. He is a throwback to the Philistines who sheared Samson. Seems that my hair bothers him. More than that, he can equate long hair with sin, riots, Communists (not that he ever saw a Chinese Communist with long side burns), and all kinds of evil. He said that You couldn't use a preacher with long side burns. He also had a few things to say about the religious value of burr hair cuts.

Apparently there are still people running around in Your Name judging people by the outward appearance. Judging, condemning, fault finding and pushing burr hair cuts all in the Name of Jesus.

Lord, have mercy upon us. We are determined to change grace and love into law and condemnation.

Mary Ellen

I try to understand people. And I try to
understand myself enough not to over react or
shoot from the hip. At times I seem to progress.
At times I am more patient. At least I make some
progress until I have a run in with Mary Ellen.

Mary Ellen rubs me raw. She irritates me.
Aggravates me. Makes me mad. And she knows it.

Mary Ellen has been a church member for
years and years. She is past fifty. Married to a
fine man. He is a Deacon in the church. He has a
good job and travels a lot. Probably travels so that
he won't have to be at home with Mary Ellen. He
doesn't really do much in or for the church. The
people elect him because they feel sorry for him
and because they don't want to get Mary Ellen
upset.

Mary Ellen never loses her cool. She never puts
anyone down to their face. She is snide. Makes
caustic remarks about people. Finds fault. She is
an investigator by nature. Always probing,
questioning, prying. She is skilled at innuendo,
suggestive remarks, and unfinished sentences. She
smiles and smirks at the wrong time. No one
feels easy or comfortable around Mary Ellen.

A long time ago I learned that Mary Ellen was
usually the origin of most problems in the church.
When people have "heard" something, they usually
"heard" it from Mary Ellen. When someone was
hurt, the hurt usually came from Mary Ellen.

I've had it out with Mary Ellen a dozen times. I've lost my temper with her. Told her off. It never does any good — she just smirks at me, and then tells everyone what an intemperate rascal I am. Mary Ellen and I can't get along.

This morning she faces serious, very serious, surgery. I'm on my way to pray with Mary Ellen, and I wanted to be honest with You Lord, in this prayer before I go pray a public prayer with Mary Ellen.

The Poet

He says that he is a poet. Being a poet is more than making rhyme. More than ordering words into stately sound and marked sequence. More than creating rhythm and measure. I read some of his poetry. It has the lilt of children laughing and the gasp of anticipation. It is sometimes the sigh of melancholy and the groan of pain. It is sometimes dull and without meaning to the reader, but profound and expressive to the writer.

But he means more by "poet" than the verse he writes. He is a sensitive man. Too sensitive. He hears sounds that others do not hear and they may not be sounds at all. He sees sights others do not see, and they may not be sights at all. He feels things that others do not feel and I think his feelings are authentic.

His values are different. He was a hippie before there were hippies. He didn't care about money, banks, titles, and shoes. He did not have ambition, drive, and the urge to succeed. He did not seek approval or promotion. He did not buy cars, or purchase life insurance, or punch time clocks.

He was not acquainted with gossip, nor did he talk about war, politics, and economics. In fact, his conversation is not very interesting. Who wants to talk about flowers, love, and sunsets?

I know him as a lonely man who wants to write, climb hillsides, collect rocks and watch birds. A lonely man who enjoys museums, concerts, art shows, and classical music.

His wife doesn't care about the things he cares about. His two sons enjoy athletics, promotions in the factory, and sex. The people who live in his neighborhood think he is nuts.

And I don't really understand him, don't even like him very well. But he is one of Your children. A lonely child. And I pray for him.

Probation?

Seems that problems accumulate for some people. I've known W. J. for several years. His wife attended our church and brought the little girls to Sunday School. W. J. always said he was too busy to come to church. Oh, he was friendly enough, courteous, never hostile or critical of the church. He liked to talk and usually talked about himself.

I read in the paper that he had been indicted by the Grand Jury. He was in trouble on several counts, mostly questionable business deals. His wife said he was innocent. He said that he was framed. His attorney said that he was guilty of bad judgement and had a desire to be a big shot. The Grand Jury said that he was a crook.

At his request I sat through the trial. I decided that he really wasn't guilty of criminal behaviour, but he did use bad judgement. He was greedy and he did want to be a big shot. While the trial was going on he was arrested for speeding, not that speeding was so serious, but he tried to fight with the policeman.

The Jury found him guilty. While waiting an appeal, he got drunk and was arrested again. More trouble.

In the middle of this turmoil, he started coming to church. He made a decision and was baptized. He is around the church every time the door is open. He is working regularly and is paying off some debts. He isn't drinking. His wife says that his attitude about everything is better. She believes that he has truly been converted. His life has been changed by Your Power. I believe that, too.

Now it's time for his appeal to be heard. The Judge has to decide whether to sentence him to the penitentiary, probate him, or perhaps even dismiss the case. I'm a little tense about it, Lord. I like W. J. I like his wife and kids. I believe that he has changed.

We need Your intervention in this situation, Lord.

Another Billy Graham

As you know I spent some time today with a young evangelist. He is in his middle twenties and is very impressive. Has an open countenance, boundless enthusiasm, good use of words, and a contagious exuberance about life and his ministry. Seems like I am so often with cynical, tired, and defeated people. It was refreshing to be with this young zealot.

He has been very successful in evangelism. His meetings attract large crowds — very large crowds! When he gives the invitation, people pour down the aisles to the altar. People buy his books. They want his picture. He has sermons on records and tapes and people buy the recordings.

He is followed around by an entourage of attractive and devoted young people. They seem to reverence him. They want to wait on him hand and foot. He is kind and thoughtful of his adoring disciples. He is not patronizing.

His team travels all over the nation. He conducts meetings in the large cities, is written up in the daily papers, has his name plastered on bill boards and is interviewed on the T.V. talk shows. He is living an exciting life. Apparently there are no financial problems.

This is a heady potion for a young preacher. Once upon a time, Father, I was a young preacher. And, I'll remind You that this kind of life had mighty appeal to me. Today I remembered how I felt in my middle twenties when I wondered if I would be the next Billy Graham. That's exactly what the young evangelist is thinking. He thinks he will be the next Billy Graham.

He may be. At least he has a better start than I had at his age. A better start than thousands, I suppose, who have had the same dream. He is honest, open, and sincere. Maybe he is the one, or maybe there will not be another national evangelist. But that is up to You. I did enjoy meeting the young man.

For Courage

Courage isn't tough talk or fist fights or charging the enemy lines. It isn't a free-fall parachute jump or washing windows on a skyscraper, or going down in a submarine or riding a rocket to the moon. Not that people who do these things are not courageous, but their risky living doesn't necessarily mean courage.

I pray for courage to accept myself without role playing or pretending. Courage to accept myself without decoration or stupid self-esteem. Courage to think and act within the limits and potentials of my own being.

I pray for courage to accept failure — to accept failure without blaming someone else. To accept failure without finding fault with those who share my failure — without condemning and hurting others. To accept failure without giving up — without losing self-confidence and self-respect.

I pray for courage to endure pain — the pain of physical illness and disability — the pain of loneliness. I pray for courage to endure being misunderstood and being prejudged. To endure the pain of criticism. Help me to accept pain without becoming bitter, self-centered, and angry.

I pray for courage to persevere. It's so easy to quit — to quit in frustration and despair. It takes courage to run the entire race, to climb all of the mountain, to cross the entire river, to finish an assignment, to maintain loyalty to the end.

I pray for courage to love. This may be the most difficult thing of all. We all have loved and lost. We give our love to people who do not return love, or they misuse our love, or they destroy our love. Lord, give me courage to love. Not just my family. That kind of love is easy and natural, but courage to love people who may distort my love.

Lord, give me courage.

The Old Preacher Died

I went to a funeral the other day. It made a lasting impression on me. This old preacher died. He's been preaching for fifty-six years. Served one church for thirty-five years. His wife has been gone for more than thirty years and had left him to raise eight children. By Your Grace, he raised them well. All eight finished college.

The old preacher was a Negro.

Now You know more about him than I do, but it must have been tough, exceedingly tough, for a Negro to put eight kids through college back in the thirties. There wasn't much money around, especially for black preachers, and not many schools to choose from. It was before affluence, before "equal" job opportunities, before integrated schools.

Four of his sons followed him into the ministry. In fact, that is why I went to the funeral. I know those sons. They are unusual men in their own right. Alert. Committed. Capable. Influential. Another son was the first black man to earn a Ph.D. in a Kentucky University. He could be proud of his children.

Another thing impressed me. More than 60 black preachers were at the funeral. He had been a kind of hero to the younger ones, a friend and co-worker with the older ones. They were there to pay tribute to a fallen brother and to precious memories of another day. I guess all of them, like me, wondered if that many preachers would ever care when they are gone.

The choir sang. There were 92 choir singers. It was a moving experience hearing 92 choir singers. They praised You and were thankful for the old preacher.

So, I'm thankful tonight for this old preacher. He touched people with a tender hand. Somehow this man had achieved what most of us want. A good family, a good name, and a triumphant death.

And I'm glad I went to his funeral.

My Brother

There was a time in the church when our religious ancestors called one another "Brother" and "Sister". It was a part of the tradition. Then they began attaching "Brother" to the clergy. Priests, preachers, and pastors were called "Brother" as a kind of title. Because titles of any kind are suspect in this generation, we rarely use the word "Brother" in a religious context. Occasionally we talk about brotherhood, but we don't talk much about brothers.

I notice, too, that people don't call You "Father" much, either. When they talk about You they use other titles, some of them are very biblical and some very flowery. When people pray, they don't call You "Father". They say a lot of things in their prayers, some very eloquent, some very emotional, and some are very repetitious. But not many prayers sound like a child talking to a Father.

Maybe we do not have many good models. Maybe we don't have enough earthly examples of brotherly love and fatherly care. Maybe we have such fragile family ties that we are incapable of visualizing brothers and fathers. Maybe the dissolution of family love has also perverted our concepts of the religious family.

Anyway, today a fifteen year old black boy in our church passed me in the lobby of a bank building. He is a tall, chocolate brown football player. Lives with a crippled mother and four younger sisters. They live on welfare in the deteriorating inner city. His mother is an alcoholic. A few months ago I baptized this young man.

Today when we met he smiled and said "Good Morning, Brother". I liked that — Father.

A Problem

I have a problem that doesn't improve. Contrary to what most people think, I'm not turned off by people who behave badly. I can understand and sympathize with people who have moral problems — the alcoholic, the gambler, the criminal, the adulterer. I can feel something for these people. I can tolerate them — try to help them.

My problem is with the super-religious people. The people who talk about the Bible all of the time. The ones who always have some new insight. The super-spiritual people who talk about their prayer life — who boast about their piety. The ones who think that their way is the only way.

They predicate everything by saying that You have told them, or that You said, or that You did something else. They have some special relationship with You — at least that's what they say.

Maybe I am uncomfortable around these people because they are better than I am. Perhaps I feel guilty in their presence. I do not talk as much about the Bible, prayer, and the Holy Ghost as these people do. They make me uncomfortable.

Maybe I, too, am smug. I think it is wrong and hypocritical to parade piety. I think that a constant conversation about piety turns people off. Consequently it is easy for me to be critical, and at that point I think I become self-righteous.

It is always tough for us to get along with other people. It is hard to accept people like they are without being judgemental and self-serving. It is difficult to tolerate errors and it is equally difficult to tolerate self-righteousness. Loving our neighbor is not an easy assignment, especially when he is a religious bore. Deliver me from the irritation and impatience that I feel about the super-religious.

Comparison

My friend was saying, "Just compare your church to some of the other churches in town. Why, your church is larger. You have more members, more buildings, more money and more programs than nearly any other church of any denomination. You should be glad that you are not Pastor of another church". And, of course, by that standard of comparison my friend is right. Comparing one church to another church can be revealing.

It's like talent. I know a teen-age baseball player who is the best player on his team. He hits better, throws better, runs better, and fields better than any other player on his team. By that standard of comparison he is doing well. I personally think that he is like my church though, he is not living up to his potential and his standards are too low.

It's like a family. The kids don't run away from home. The husband and wife don't fight or threaten divorce. The family isn't like a lot of other families that quarrel, alienate and eventually dissolve. But it is not really sensible to make that kind of comparison. A family should try to reach the level of joy and happiness that they have the potential to reach.

Lord, we're always playing that game and falling into that kind of trap. We have learned to excuse any kind of failure, mistake or sin by saying "Well, I know of people who are sorrier than I am." It's always true, too. There is always someone more wicked, someone more arrogant, someone more selfish. There is always someone who makes us look good by comparison.

I'm thinking tonight of the Pharisee who thanked God that he wasn't like the Publican.

Please help me not to play that game, but to
find a higher standard.

The Run Away

I've known the Grants for more than ten years.
I've watched Lucian grow up. He's about fifteen
now. He is built tall and thin. Fair complexion.
His face is pretty — too pretty to be a boy's face.
He has long hair that looks like his sisters.
He imitates his sisters.

Lucian is terribly shy and self-conscious. He is
awkward, and nearly incoherent around adults.
He doesn't have friends. He isn't interested in
parties, or ball games, or dates.

For a long time some of us have been aware of
his problems and knew that these social problems
would increase as he grew older. And the problems
did increase.

Funny thing! Our social problems and personal
problems are all tied up together. The way we get
along with other people reveals what we think of
ourselves. When we are dissatisfied with what we
are, we invariably withdraw from others, as if
isolation will cure us — as if self-respect can be
found in solitude.

It's not that Lucian was or is hostile to other
people. He doesn't start arguments. He doesn't
pick fights. He isn't abrasive, or rude, or touchy.

He just ignores people. Hides away from them. Misses school. Stays in his room. Prefers to eat alone. Sits by himself in church — when he comes to church. When his parents have guests he hides away in another room.

Yesterday he ran away from home. We thought he would come home last night. But he didn't.

Somewhere out there tonight there is a frail little boy who can't fit in anywhere. He doesn't like people and he doesn't like himself.

But he is one of Your children, Lord. Protect him and bring him home. We'll try to do better by Lucian.

It Doesn't Seem Fair

Last week a thief stole $500 worth of stuff off our church buses. Wonder why they didn't steal it off a beer truck? An arsonist burned our church buildings to the ground a couple of years ago. I can't help but wonder why they didn't burn a brothel or a brewery. Sometimes it doesn't seem fair.

Two girls were mangled up in an auto wreck. One of the girls had a brother killed in an auto wreck last year and the other girl lost a brother in Viet Nam. And, as I sit with these broken-hearted parents who still have a fresh pain from the deaths of their sons, I don't think it's fair.

A saintly old woman lives in anguish and indescribable pain, neglected and dying, in a nursing home. A mafia type hoodlum on our street enjoys good health and has an entourage of friends. A little boy is crippled, another one is retarded, and there is a blind little boy in our church. Other little boys play ball, and it doesn't seem fair.

All my life I've seen good people get hurt — mistreated. I'm all too familiar with pain, with loss, with suffering, with neglect! Everything in my heart protests pain and hurt. I want things to be fair. I expect a balance. I think that life should compensate.

At precisely this point I must pray. There are things I can't change. I'm not strong enough, or wise enough, or good enough to be judge. I am not able, or willing to run the show. I don't keep score like You do. I don't see it like You do. I admit that Your ways and my ways are not the same. So with some hesitancy, and even doubt, I bow again to pray "Thy Will Be Done".

But I must be honest enough to let You know tonight, that sometimes things don't seem fair. I trust You, though!

Deliver Us From Evil

I was in a meeting today and everyone repeated the Lord's Prayer. This is one of those ceremonial rituals we perform that is a kind of hat tipping to You. That's o.k. I guess You would rather we tip our hat than ignore You completely. It is at least a courtesy.

Who am I to judge? Maybe those people really prayed the Lord's Prayer and meant every single word they said.

But it struck me as we mumbled through the ancient prayer. That part "Deliver Us From Evil" struck me, Lord.

I guess we all have some pretty clear ideas about evil. We can describe or catalogue evils. Murder! Rape! Child abuse! Theft! Hate! Greed! Lying! In fact, given time, we could make a real long list of evil — sins — transgressions.

Oh, I realize that none of us wants to commit murder and be arrested and be hanged. We don't want the consequences of evil. We don't want to be punished. Even small children learn right from wrong, and they don't want to get caught.

But I'm not sure that we want to be delivered from evil either, Father.

I have a feeling that we kind of like evil. Not horrible, bizarre things. But we all like to break the rules. We actually enjoy and are kind of fascinated by sin.

So this business of deliverance from evil does, in fact, go against the grain. We better pray that part of the Lord's Prayer with a little more thought. We might be surprised if we really were delivered from evil. Surprised and changed.

rustrations

They just won't do what I say.
My advice and counsel
Seems to be right —
But they refuse.

It appeared to be going O.K.
Pieces were being put together.
Something broken was mended —
But it broke again.

What difference do I really make?
Who responds?
Who listens?
Who cares?

They try, they honestly try, they want to —
But there is no way out.
No light in the tunnel.
It will not get better.

There are those things and those people
That are beyond my influence.
Some things I can't handle —
But I still believe!

Lily Rose

Lily Rose has been married ten times. Not twice.
Not five times. Not eight times. But, ten times
Lily Rose has promised "till death do us part".
She is a female counterpart to King Solomon.
Every marriage ends in divorce. I guess she holds
some kind of local record for failures.

Lily Rose, she says that her name makes her
the original flower child, is about forty — give or
take a couple of years. She isn't coarse or vulgar.
She looks young and fresh. She is reasonably
intelligent and reasonably pretty. She isn't loud.
She isn't offensive. In fact, she has some attractive
personality traits.

I've known Lily Rose for four or five years, or
four or five husbands. She comes by the office to
talk. Never about a marital problem, always about
her son. A little seven year old boy.

She has successfully separated her marital
exploits from this child's problems. I honestly
believe that she has conditioned herself to believe
that her messed up concepts of marriage have no
effects on the child. She apparently doesn't relate
the little boys deficiencies to her own bizarre
behaviour. At least she doesn't admit the
relationship.

I've tried, I've really tried, to get her on base.
She simply cannot raise a normal son with this
constant procession of husbands and changing
fathers. The little fellow is insecure, afraid, and

confused. There is no stability and very little love in his home. I feel sorry for him and want to help. But how can I help the little boy when his mother needs help and won't admit it?

It's not that Lily Rose is so wicked. I'm not mad at her. But she is so insensitive. She behaves so stupidly. She is so frustrating. And the little boy is losing.

How can we get Lily Rose to settle down?

The Children and School Busing

It has often been said that old men plan wars for young men to fight. Viet Nam was our longest national war and the young men who fought when it began are now older men. I guess old men do use young men to fight their wars.

If Americans were upset about Viet Nam, they are more upset about school busing to achieve racial balance. Now this national controversy has erupted in our city and in our church. It's an unpleasant experience.

I'm inclined to pray tonight for the children involved. I have a reasonable conviction that the children are being used. They are being used by a government that assumes that they know what is right for the child and the parent doesn't know best. They are being used by courts that decree that racial balance is the same as quality education. The children are being used by unhappy white and black adults who have more prejudice than judgement. The children are being moved around like chess pawns to satisfy certain adult desires.

Now don't misunderstand. I know that some schools are sorry. The buildings are bad. Curriculum is limited, teachers are poor, and more often than not the sorry school is the one largely populated by blacks.

I want the kids to have an equal chance. Not a separate but equal chance. But an equal educational chance.

The way things are going around here today, the children seem to be forgotten. People, adult people, are threatening, cursing, going to court and conducting demonstrations. It's ugly and serious.

Just seems to me that no one is really thinking about the children. And there is precious little that I can do about it but pray. I don't even know what to pray for except the kids. Come to think of it, that's more than enough.

Church Finance

I've known for a long time that nothing can agitate and upset a congregation more than money.

I try real hard not to become a financial administrator, or fund raiser, or collection taker, or a religious huckster.

But it takes money to operate the church. I know that churches waste a lot of money. Some of it is stupid waste. Some deliberate.

Actually, though, my conscience is pretty clear on this score. I honestly believe that we are careful and generous in our spending — fair and honest in collecting. We give away a lot and that's the way it should be.

Anyhow, my problem tonight is James. He is that one church member who talks the most about spending. He criticizes what we do with money. He's always suspicious of the finance committee. He finds fault with the budget. He questions motives and methods. He wants to pass church rules that would force everyone to tithe. He irritates me!

He reported his contributions on his Income Tax return and they checked him out with the church financial secretary. Seems that James is a liar. A cheat. He gives about $5.00 a week to the church and has stretched that amount on his tax report to $25.00.

He was frightened and apparently is going to settle it up with the government privately. But now I know that he is a liar.

It's going to be hard for me to keep my tongue with James. Hard to listen to him. Hard to even be around him. The Lord will have to help me.

Can A Man Change?

I have an internal conflict. I wonder how much, if any, a person can change. This conflict is accented because of the occupation I'm in.

A lot of marriage counseling pivots around this question. Women marry men and try to change them. Men try to change their wives. Parents smother kids and try to make the children into something they're not. We recognize the diversity of individuals. We talk about accepting and loving people as they are. We should be able to help people without insisting on change. This seems to be the way God accepts us.

At the same time we try, through the church, to bring about change in people. We try to help them overcome weakness and selfishness. We talk about conversion, new creations, new birth and things like that. Part of our evangelical tradition is changed living.

We also talk about growth and maturity. We expect people to grow up, accept responsibility, conform, behave, and act in acceptable ways. No one can completely do his own thing. We are perplexed by selfishness, by immaturity. All of this has to do with change.

Tonight, I'm thinking about the woman whose husband has left her. She says that if he will come home, she will change. I'm thinking about the young husband in jail for the third time this year. He says that when he gets out he will change. I'm thinking of the teenager who says he will change if given another chance. I'm thinking of a whole procession of people — alcoholics, complainers, cheats, liars, haters, and schemers who want, always want, a chance to change.

And I know people who have changed, have been changed. And I know people who never change. It is confusing.

Another Baby

Perhaps the most private decision that a husband and wife make is about birth control or planned parenthood. Some people think this is a purely religious question and they reason that no one has children that God doesn't send. They figure that the purpose of marriage is to have children. They are taught this by parents and church.

I guess that it is really up to the man and woman. They can decide when and how many kids they want and can care for.

Anyway, I'm thinking tonight about this mother. Her name is Mary Lee. She has four children. The last two have been handicapped. Retarded in mind, deformed in body. The retarded child comes to our church.

Mary Lee is pregnant again. It's been seven years since she had a baby. She's past forty now. She is scared to death that this new baby will be retarded, or crippled, or that something will be

121

wrong. She thinks she is too old to have a new baby — and she may be. She says that they can't afford another baby. She says that the two handicapped children won't be able to cope with the new baby.

I've talked with her two or three times. Today she talked about an abortion. Also talked about her sanity. Says she thinks she will lose her mind.

Her husband won't talk about it. Won't talk to her about it. Won't talk to me about it. Won't talk to the doctor. He says only that God sends babies and He is sending this one and He may send a dozen more.

I have a feeling that Mary Lee is more upset about her husband's neglect and insensitivity than she is about the pregnancy. But that's just a feeling, she never says it.

Well, I'm not sure about this at all. I don't think Mary Lee will crack. She may. I think I'm opposed to abortions. I think her husband is treating her badly. It's a tough one. I know the Lord wants to help her — and her husband — and this unwanted baby.

Tony

This happens too often. The girl's name is Tony. She will be a senior in high school. At least that's what I thought, what her parents thought, and what her friends thought. But she won't be in high school this year. She is pregnant. Another unmarried mother.

We talked and she told me the alternatives as she sees them.

She can go out of state and have an abortion. She knows some girls that have gone to New York. Most of them came out of it o.k. One of them was seriously ill when she came back. Infection. Another one has had some emotional problems and is under psychiatric care. Tony thinks she would feel guilty. She thinks the unborn child is a human.

Tony also has thought about going to a home for unwed mothers and then letting the baby out for adoption. She thinks that people would find out where she has been. She thinks this is a cop out and that she would feel guilty about that, too.

The child's father is an immature boy. He isn't ready for marriage. He and Tony don't love one another. She is horrified at the thought of being married to him and having him as the father of the child. But he is the father and he doesn't want to marry either. She says that there is no reason to give the baby his name when he doesn't want the baby and he doesn't want her.

Tony has thought about having the baby and not getting married. She realizes that the baby will grow up with a stigma. It probably wouldn't be fair to the baby.

Well, there is never an easy or pleasant way to solve this kind of problem. Tony does have alternatives but none of them are agreeable.

123

Maybe the Lord can help her make the right choice and to endure the consequences of any choice — if she'll let Him.

The Young Preacher

The young man has been in our church since he was ten or eleven. He has a good mind, if not a brilliant mind. He accepts responsibility reasonably well, although there are evidences of erratic and emotional behaviour. He gets along with people fairly well, but he doesn't excel with people. His parents are average people and more than average church members. The young man is in his first year of college and has decided he wants to be a pastor. He says that he has been "called".

This is difficult for me. It has always been difficult for me. I have preacher friends who steadily produce young preachers. I've never had that kind of record or reputation. Privately I've wondered about it. I've wondered if young men have failed to consider the ministry because of the way I conduct my ministry. After all, I'm the only pastor a generation of those young men have known.

I attach great importance to vocation. I believe that a person who makes the right marriage choice and the right vocational choice is about assured of a happy and successful life. The wrong choices in a job or a mate invariably mean unhappiness and insecurity.

A choice for the ministry has a lot of finality to it. The ministry is so complex and tense. It has changed so much and still changes in abrupt and unpleasant ways. The ministry today is not very much like the vocation I went into twenty-six years ago.

It just seems so important and so personal to me. Consequently it's hard for me to encourage or discourage this young man. I really don't know how to help him decide. It really ends up where it should, I suppose. It is his decision.

He Wants To Preach

The man says that he's been called into the ministry. He came to me for some advice. I found out that he doesn't want advice, he wants approval. More than approval, he wants a church job.

This is always an awkward kind of situation for me. I do not know what a person really feels and I can't determine their motives. For years I've seen this happen. Not many of them follow through on their "call". Again, maybe some of them would follow through if I were more sympathetic and helpful.

The fellow today is past thirty. Married with three children. He hasn't been in the church very long, in fact he hasn't been a Christian very long.

As far as I can see he has no particular gifts for the ministry. He hasn't executed much leadership in the church so far. His training is even more limited than his skills. I do not doubt his sincerity. I do not doubt that men are called to serve.

But I'm reluctant to encourage a man to announce publicly that he is going into the ministry when there are so many obvious obstacles. Changing jobs and starting school will be tough for him and his family. Assuming he finishes school, I'm not sure that he has much to contribute to a church as a paid worker. I'm not sure that a church will employ him.

Perhaps that is not my worry.

It's hard for me to deceive myself or the man. I am simply not enthusiastic or pleased about this. He knew it. He read me and it hurt his feelings. He is disappointed. He thought that I would be excited and delighted.

Realize that I'm judging his ability, and I'm sure that I'm questioning his judgement. I have mixed-up feelings. I don't want to pass judgement and I don't want to encourage a good man in a mistake.

Shooting From The Hip

My friend has gotten out on a limb. He didn't intend to get into this kind of bind. He came into a meeting tired. He works hard and had too little sleep for too many nights. He looked tired. He was tired. He and his wife had a spat at the dinner table. This was unusual and unexpected because they get along well and they love one another. But they argued in anger.

So he left his house to attend the church meeting. Tired and angry. Angry at himself for cutting his wife with harsh words. By the time he got to the church he was filled with remorse and disgust.

The church meeting was too long, as church meetings are inclined to be. Some of it was important. Some was trivial. One of the men, Sam, sets people on edge. Sam is self-righteous. He puts people down. He talks too much. He brags about his piety. He is very critical of other people and will not yield the floor. Sam is enamored with himself, but we all know Sam and expect to hear him out.

But last night my friend, tired and angry, couldn't take Sam. He interrupted Sam. He didn't criticize Sam. He criticized all of us. Said he wasn't ever coming back to the church. Said he didn't believe in the church any more or in God for that matter. He shocked the men. Shocked me. Most of all he shocked and surprised himself.

Now he is hung up. When he stalked out of the meeting he went to my office. Sat there waiting for me. Apologized to me. Said that he was tired. Told me about his spat with his wife. Said that someone needed to put Sam in his place. He admitted that he had shot from the hip. We had a good talk and I expected him back at church Sunday, but he didn't show.

He is embarrassed. His pride is hurt. I feel for him.

The Other Cheek

I read these articles about how to overcome opposition. About how to get along with disagreeable people. How to act when people hurt you. All of this reads well. In fact I give out a lot of that kind of advice myself.

Everyone runs into conflict. We have it in the churches. There is dissension on ball teams. Secretaries hassle in the offices. Tension mounts in factories and on assembly lines. Parents and their children argue and fuss. I guess husbands and wives have more conflict than is encountered in any other relationship.

At times we all expect opposition. Certain people expect it as a way of life, politicians for instance. Other people are antagonistic, belligerent and hyper-sensitive and they incur hostility and antagonism.

But a lot of times we get into conflicts inadvertantly. Totally unexpectedly. We are not prepared for the opposition. We think it is unfair — illogical — unreasonable. At least it seems to be unreasonable.

That's my problem tonight. Davis is sore at me. He started out with a few sarcastic remarks. Then we were in a meeting together and he made some criticisms and accusations that didn't make sense — at least they didn't seem sensible to me. I overreacted. Reacted in anger. Forced a confrontation with him. Then I backed down because I wasn't out to hurt him. He interpreted my backing down and acquiescence as agreement or weakness. Maybe it was weakness.

Now he is really on my back. Others are involved. Others will be hurt. I would turn the other cheek again if that would help the situation. Would it help? Would it help him? I don't know!

Paying the Preacher

One of the things that I dislike the most about my job is budget time. I don't like to "raise" money for anything. I guess I always wish that people would give their money to worthy causes and to the church without pressure and promotion, but they won't do it that way. People are not inherently generous and are not spontaneous in their giving.

My salary comes out of the church budget, which means that when I urge the people to support the church budget, I'm urging them to help pay my salary. Of course every businessman in America tries to sell his merchandise or services to put money in his pocket and that is acceptable and expected. But it is distasteful to me to try to collect money.

When the Budget Committee meets they discuss all of the expenses of the church: Missions, radio/T.V., electric bills, literature and more than one hundred other line items in the budget. Then they get to salaries and I get up tight. They're good men. They are conscientous. They try to be fair.

But the salary isn't determined by normal criteria. I'm not sure how other salaries are determined. Hours? Training? Experience? Effectiveness? Cost of living? Replacement cost? I'm not sure how churches determine salaries, either. After 25 years as a paid pastor, I really don't know how they decide.

Some of them think that the pastor should be poor. Some think he shouldn't be paid more than they are paid. Some want to pay him based on their liking him. Some think it depends upon the church income. Some see him as a professional. Some think he is a hired hand. Some think his work is important. Some think it is unimportant. Some think he wastes money.

So it's budget time and people sit down to decide what to pay the preacher. I'm not complaining. I don't know of any better way to do it. They give the money, but it is always embarrassing for me. At times I think my work is worth more than they can ever pay. At other times I think they are too generous. So be it.

Peter's Past

A lot of people give my name as a reference. They normally do this when they are changing jobs, or perhaps when they are trying to adopt a child. Sometimes political candidates want me to endorse them, or someone will do some work or service for me and they want to use me as a reference.

I guess this is all-right as long as it represents my opinion and my judgement. Usually I don't think it makes much difference, anyway. At least it doesn't make much difference if I don't have any strong negative opinions.

Now today I'm faced with a dilemma.

This man, Peter, is a member of our church. When he first came to the church he told me that he had some problems with bad checks. Later on he admitted to me, without my asking, that he had also been arrested twice for shoplifting. Everytime he had paid off the bad checks and paid for the things he had stolen. He usually spent three or four days in jail and that was the limit of his punishment.

He is married and has two sons. He is apparently a fairly dependable factory worker. He gets along reasonably well with his wife and his little boys love him. He attends church regularly and seems sincere about his church jobs and his religion.

Peter wants to change jobs. Says that he wants to better himself. One of the church men is considering hiring him. The prospective employer

is a good friend of mine. He is a responsible man.
Peter will be handling money. He asked me if he
could trust Peter. He doesn't know that Peter has
had problems.

Should I tell him about Peter's past? Somehow
I just don't trust Peter. Maybe I'm too suspicious.
Maybe I'm not forgiving enough. What should I do?

Daniel

I've just never met anyone quite like Daniel.
He has a reasonably successful men's clothing
store. I'm confident that he has more business
than ever expected. He has made money and
spends it in all of the proper status ways —
overseas travel, expensive automobile, children in
private schools, large house. He creates an image
of affluence. This is important to Daniel.

Literally every time I talk with Daniel he has
some big scheme working. He is going to give up
his store, or he is going to open six more stores
just like it. He may be going to build a hotel, or a
health club, or he is going back to school and
become an attorney. He may be talking about
moving to Alaska, or Nebraska, or moving back
to the farm where he was born.

He may be planning to buy into a fried
chicken store, a barber shop, a race horse, or a
bank building. He may be talking about running
for mayor, organizing a club to preserve dogwood

and daffodils, or joining the local V.F.W. Post.
Daniel plans tours of Japan, Colombia, the Grand
Canyon, and the local IBM plant. He decides to
take flying lessons, join a bowling league, and
study cello.

Daniel is a sincere person about his religion.
He attends church services every time the door is
open...for a few weeks. Then he decides to go to
Nigeria or Mexico as a missionary, or he joins a
home prayer group, or he trys to get the gift of
tongues, or he becomes enamored with a traveling
evangelist, or he is absorbed with second-coming
prophecy.

I pray for Daniel. I like him. I think he is
basically honest and sincere. But he sure is at
loose ends. He is strung out. He is never content —
never satisfied — never really happy. He is like a
mini-whirlwind. He needs some calm.

Arthur Morris III

I spent some time today with Arthur Morris.
Arthur Morris the third, that is. That "third" bit is
the problem. The Morris family is an old family in
our area. They figure prominently in local history
and politics. They own land. They are in the
established society of the Bluegrass. They have
passed a fortune from one generation to the next,
and most generations have added to the fortune.

The Morris family has a good reputation. They

133

are honest people. The support all of the appropriate charities. They are members of the right organizations and clubs. They are important and respected people in our city. They are church people.

Arthur has already added significantly to the family wealth. He is an astute manipulator of money and land. He has been able to invest in the right thing at the right time. When people say that Arthur Morris III doesn't really know what he is worth, they are nearly correct.

So here we are with a young man of tremendous fortune, a beautiful family, a respected family tree. A man who has influence, prestige, and power in the city. He isn't greedy. He isn't sick. He isn't an alcoholic. He isn't a parasite. And he isn't happy.

Arthur Morris III says that people do not respect him as a person. He thinks that people treat him with respect because of his wealth, his name, and his power. He says that he would like for people to like him and respect him if his name was Joe Smith — if he were just a tenant, or a cab driver. He wonders if he could make it as a person just on his own personal contribution. He wonders if he has real value separated from his name and his wealth.

I don't know. I don't know many people like Arthur Morris III and I don't have his particular problem. I told him I would pray with him.

Lawson's Dilemma

I'm not sure how this situation should turn out.

Lawson has been in our church for two or three years. He has not been a popular or respected church member, although he is present every time the door is open. I think he wants friends and he really thinks that people listen to him.

He is somewhat a self-made man. He has a very limited education, but he has earned some money. He lives in a nice house and drives an expensive car. He dresses his wife and children well. He has developed an adequate vocabulary. He considers himself knowledgeable about everything and is very opinionated and argumentive about his opinions.

Lawson is very strict and very rigid about his religious opinions, and about church policy. He insists that people respond his way. He hurts people — I don't think he means to hurt them. I also don't think he cares if he hurts them — he is insensitive.

Very slowly it dawned on me that Lawson was changing. He was more hostile and critical. More aggressive in his opinions. About this same time I began to have some suspicions about Lawson and Edna. Edna is married to a very weak, unattractive man. Edna has been involved with other men — at least there is evidence that she has been involved. Over the past few weeks it is obvious that Lawson is taken with Edna. Some of the people are talking.

So here it is. Lawson, who has always been

rigid and inflexible, who has always been arrogant and self-righteous, is in a bind. A scandal whirls around his head. Again, I'm not sure about him. His pattern is normally to ignore the response and reaction of other people. He may not know, or care, what people say or think. Of course, something like this where his morals are suspect might completely destroy him. And, he may be so infatuated with Edna that the opinions of others don't make any difference.

I don't know where I fit into the picture — if at all.

The Hustler

Mason was a hustler. A hustler in the classic sense of the term. He has won as much as eight hundred dollars shooting pool in an afternoon. He was so adept with the pool stick that only a few people would try him, and they had to be half drunk.

He held a regular job. Never missed work. Provided for his family. He was respected by his children, and loved by his wife. The people he worked for didn't know about his outside income. It was cash. No taxes. No reports. Easy money for Mason.

Mason got converted and joined the church. He decided that he would quit hustling. No more gambling of any kind. He has stuck to it, I believe. He acts like a changed man. Talks like a changed man. Has a different sense of values.

Now his hang up is restitution. There are three or four men that he has won a lot of money from. Mason would like to pay them back what he won, but he doesn't have the money. He doesn't have nearly enough money to pay them back.

He also is worried about the tax angle. He admits that part of this is fear. Uncle Sam may check him out. Fine him. Send him to prison. And what about his kids? Would they understand if they found out that he had collected a lot of money from gambling? He has cheated the government and the rest of the tax payers.

Getting converted is one thing. Trying to change the past is another. I pray for Mason. He has some tough decisions to make.

Two Funerals

I conducted two funerals today. This is never an easy assignment and two in one day is tiring. It puts me on an emotional pendulum. I always wonder if what I say really makes any difference or if I'm just a participant in the ritual of death.

My relationship with both families is fragile. This isn't surprising, because I discovered that both families have a lot of fragile ties.

The old lady was active and alert right up to the time of her death. She died out in the yard weeding a flower bed. Four-score years and four. She apparently had enjoyed life. Stayed busy. Read. Watched T.V. Traveled. Had friends. Owned some property.

Her children had neglected her or at least two of three children had. The daughter was attentive to her mother.

One of the sons was drunk at the funeral and was arguing with the mortician about funeral costs.

No one in this family grieved much. They didn't have much to say about their mother. Not much to say to one another. The seemed relieved when the funeral was over.

The other funeral was for an elderly man. He had died as an alcoholic. That's the way he lived. There were about ten mourners and two sons. The sons were embarrassed. They apparently don't get along with one another and hadn't seen their father for a long time. I think they were glad when that funeral was over.

Now I feel pity, helplessness, and frustration. It seems that even the common humanity so often evident at funerals is fragile, too.

I'm tired, Lord.

Hamilton

In spite of some current thought, people do change. Of course those of us who talk about conversion say that people change. We preach that men can become new creatures, with new minds, new motivation, and new life. We preach that men can be changed for the better.

Some men change and head the other direction. My friend, Hamilton, is changing for the worse. He is extremely irritable. Finds fault with other people and is constantly carping and complaining. He picks at people and puts them down. Rarely, if ever, does he smile or seem happy. He boasts about his achievements, is intolerant of anyone who differs with him and is arrogant about his opinions.

Hamilton is losing friends. His prestige and influence in the church and community is deteriorating. His own children are uncomfortable with him.

There are several things that can happen that produce this kind of change in a man. Sometimes sheer fatigue will wear a man down until he becomes abrasive. Hamilton works hard and is very ambitious. He is greedy for money and enjoys earning money, although he doesn't seem to enjoy the things money can buy.

Family problems can gradually grind a man down. A nagging wife. An incompatible marriage. Or it may be frustration about growing children. His mother is old and sick and he is edgy about her condition. All of these things are evidence of Hamilton's advancing age and he may be resisting age.

Usually when a man changes like Hamilton has, it is the product of some unresolved guilt — some kind of sin that keeps bugging him. I have a strong feeling that Hamilton needs to confess something and he needs to feel forgiven. If I'm right, how can I tell him?

A Tragedy

The woman is just thirty-eight. Her body is bloated and swollen. Her skin is so tight that it looks like it will burst like a balloon. There is one broken place on her left arm — an ugly sore that drains a stinking, thick fluid. Her skin is blotted and patched with purple and red marks.

She is bleeding from one ear and the blood has stuck to her hair. Her hair is coarse and matted, she apparently hasn't washed her head for weeks. Her teeth are yellow and her nose is swollen and distorted. Her lips are thick and dry. There are blisters on her upper lip. Her color is a dull yellow.

I tried to talk to her. She could hear me but her eyes wouldn't focus. They wandered by me. Her eyes are fearful. Not dull, but frightened. I think she can hear me but she is unresponsive. Her speech is muffled and incoherent. She speaks frantically, but it doesn't make sense.

She is probably dying.

Twelve years ago she began drinking heavily. I knew her at that time. Four children at home. She wasn't a beauty queen, but she was an attractive young lady. She had reasonable intelligence and made friends easily. People liked her and she seemed to be happy. Busy with four children, but happy. She didn't complain, attended church, enjoyed music, and seemed O.K.

Her husband left her four years ago. He had run her through two or three clinics for alcoholics. Doctors. Counselors. Me. None of us got to her. She never improved. She just kept drinking. Now she is dying.

I don't know. I don't know where we failed, if we failed, or where the failure is. But something is bad wrong. Something is sick. Ugly and sick.

Now I'll go back beside her bed and stand there with four confused, frightened, hurt children. None of us know what to do.

Ain't So Simple

As the man on television says "It ain't so simple". The longer I live the more I realize that human relations "ain't so simple". Everytime I get to the place where I feel confident and sure of my judgement something happens to humble me.

What's true in dealing with people is even more true in moral questions. Sure, some things are black and white, right and wrong. Often, perhaps most of the time, I can make a decision with some definite moral guidelines and boundaries. I've said from the pulpit that the problem isn't knowing right from wrong, it's doing what is right.

But that oversimplifies, too.

Nearly by coincidence I became involved with this highly successful young evangelist. No one can dispute his ability to preach, to impress people, and he does simply ooze with sincerity. Again, nearly by coincidence, I've helped him some with his organization. He has confided in me and we have become casual friends. I know that he is effective and I'm pragmatic enough to be impressed with anyone who gets a job done.

Now, nearly by coincidence, I've been put into close contact with a man the preacher does business with. I know this man extremely well. He is a close friend. He wants to do business with the preacher and my friend can't afford to lose money or waste time.

The preacher has a bad reputation for not paying bills. The preacher's cohorts say that he has reformed financially.

I'm not sure what I should say, if anything, to my friend who wants to do business with the preacher. I don't want either one of them hurt. As I said, "It ain't so Simple".

Easy Decisions?

One of the easiest things for preachers, church people and moralists to say is that "everything is either right or wrong." We talk about decisions of right and wrong in uncomplicated ways, often refusing to acknowledge the gray areas.

I'm praying tonight for my friend the politician. He faces a tough decision tomorrow. There is a zoning hearing coming up before his board. He will have to vote. Apparently he will cast the deciding vote because half of the board is on one side, half on the other.

Three men own some land. They have owned it for some time. They pay taxes on it. They purchased the land several years ago with the intention of building a shopping center on it. At that time, several years ago, they were promised by the incumbents that they could build the shopping center. This is a growing city. A city that apparently needed shopping centers.

But things changed. Traffic increased. Sewer problems increased. There were too many shopping centers. Poor planning and political favors allowed other kinds of building around the land in question. Opposition to the proposed center grew and solidified.

On the other hand the men do own the land. Seems like a man should be able to do what he wants with his own land—especially when he had a promise. To add to the dilemma, the developers are really good citizens. They help our city. And they are good friends of long standing with my politician friend.

So tomorrow my friend will cast a vote. It isn't easy, and he may never be sure if it was right. Every decision isn't easy.

The Rich Young Preacher

It is generally assumed that Pastors are underpaid. Usually the preacher's pay is not consistent with his education and training. Usually it is not fair considering the hours he is on call, and does not allow for the tension and responsibility of his office and duty. It is not uncommon to find pastors who really feel a financial pinch. Some of this has changed the past few years, but inflation has knocked some of those gains out.

I'm trying to keep that in mind tonight when I pray for Wayne, my pastor friend. Wayne has been a pastor for a long time now. He has always received a mediocre salary. But things have changed for Wayne. He has discovered, or been discovered, by one of these get rich pyramid selling organizations. He is selling and selling, recruiting and persuading, and he is making money! He says that he is making more than $1200.00 a week.

I don't really mind Wayne making money and I doubt that the Lord minds, either. There is no virtue in poverty. There is no evil in wealth. My concern about Wayne is personal. He is absolutely possessed and driven by this thing. When he sees a person, he sees a potential investor. Everyone is a prospect for money. He has forgotten how to see people as individuals. I'm extremely uncomfortable with him. He acts like a con-man. I guess he is.

Wayne is using his pastoral office to sell his questionable product. People had learned to trust him and respect him as a man of integrity. He is using that trust to sell his product. He talks about selling and investing as "being God's will". He is enticing people in religious terms and, by his own admission, he is pocketing money.

Somehow I feel that Wayne has sold out. Compromised. Lost his character. I don't want to be harsh or judgemental — but it all makes me feel very uncomfortable.

Can't Sleep

I've tried for an hour or more to go to sleep. Everything is a jumble. My mind is racing from one thing to another. There are explosions inside me. My thoughts are like a speeding car out of control. I can't bring any order or sequence to my thoughts and sleep won't come to relax my body and refresh my mind.

As always when I'm too tight, too tense, too

tired, the regrets and mistakes keep crowding in. They demand attention. They beg to be acknowledged. So I recite my sins, one by one. Or ten by ten. This should bring rest. Count my sins. Confess them. Admit them. Look at them. Learn from them. Repent. Promise to do better.

Sins of speech. Talking too much. Speaking in haste and impatience. Speaking in anger. Words of envy. Words of spite.

And I remember the things that I should have done today and didn't do. Some of the omissions have accumulated from yesterday, from last week, and the week before. I have put off. Delayed. Wasted time and opportunity.

Oh, God. You know all of that. You know that I make stupid mistakes. Selfish mistakes. Mistakes that can't be changed. Hurts that can't be healed. You know that I'm dumb about things and self-centered.

And I still can't sleep.

So I begin to count my blessings. Remember the things today that were good. Not that they excuse the blunders. They don't cover up the mistakes. But there have been good things. Even some good things that I had part in. And most of the good things I didn't deserve.

Funny! Now I'm ready to rest. I guess I need to count some sins and some good things. There is enough of both.

Victories

This is the hard part of the book —
Chalking up victories.
Measuring success.
Winning.

It's easy in a ball game, or a political race
Or a contest,
To know who wins, who loses.
At least, it looks easy.
We can select the successful people
By their status and money —
Boats, salaries
Bottom line.

And the BIG churches, BIG assignments
Attendance, budget.
Degrees,
Trips to the Holy Land.

Loving your wife, Loving your kids,
Loving your work,
Admitting your limitations.
Good memories.
Being honest.
This sounds like winning to me!

Some Little Things

I'm thankful for home-made ice cream. The kind made in an old-fashioned crank freezer. You turn it and turn it, mix salt in the ice, and crank some more. It tastes good on a summer night.

I'm thankful for lightning bugs, and fireflies. They keep me company in the stillness of the night. I was remembering the times I used to chase them when suddenly my reverie was interrupted as children came rushing to chase the ones I was watching. Children still pursue fireflies.

It rained tonight. A hard, summer storm. The thunder sounded like monsters in the sky. The doors and windows rattled. The lightning was so bright that it made the house look white. The rain poured in sheets. Tomorrow the earth will look washed clean. And I left a car window down, but it really doesn't make that much difference.

A little kitten has been on the patio for three or four days. We told our little girl that the kitten couldn't stay. I've sneaked it some milk, so has my wife. My little girl has been playing with the kitten. She feeds it, talks to it, and holds it. The kitten will stay.

I read a book about Ethel Waters. Seemed like she was talking to me. She says that You know her address and she knows Your address. That's a good way to put it. That's the way Ethel Waters says it. I believe that, too. I just don't say it that way. She has had a remarkable and successful life.

Thank-you, Lord, for freezer ice cream, lightning bugs, summer storms, a kitten, Ethel Waters book, and piano music. These kinds of things are important to You, too.

The Surprising Church

Sometimes I get real impatient with my church people. They fail to support the most worthy and obvious causes. The gap between what they profess and what they practice is so wide, and they get offended over the smallest and most ridiculous things. They get excited and enthused about unimportant things. This kind of inconsistency drives preachers to the brink of despair.

On the other hand, I wonder sometimes that the church as we know it exists at all. It's continued existence is built upon the loyalty and integrity of those same people.

I'm always surprised that so many people come to church and hear what are too often sorry sermons. Not that our sermon subject is sorry, but we deliver those sermons poorly, prepare insufficiently, and preach carelessly.

I'm surprised at how much money they give away through the church. Not that many of them give enough that it makes them poor, but they do give away quite a lot when it is collected together.

I'm surprised that they get along with one

another as well as they do when I stop to realize how much tension there is in the average family, factory, or shop. When I realize how many people quarrel with their neighbors, how many people hassle with their boss, how much anger and violence there is in America, I'm just surprised that churches get along as well as they do.

Of course all of this just reminds me that the church is, in fact, God's. He gives these people some special grace, motivation and courage. And in the church these weak people, like me, seem to occasionally rise above themselves.

So tonight, Lord, I thank You again for my church. Better yet, I thank You for Your Church.

New Year's Day

I guess all of us humans need some kind of stopping place and some kind of beginning place. That's the best purpose of our New Year's Day and the kind of calendar we have. God doesn't need calendars, watches, and schedules. But we do!

We need to stop occasionally to see where we've been. Not that we have been so far or done so much, but we have travelled some distance and hopefully have made some progress. It is important that we stop for that backward look. It may put things in perspective. We can learn something from our yesterdays.

And, on the New Year, we usually try to see where we are. This is a product of where we've been. Where we are will determine where we're going.

Most of us who live by anticipation and faith can get real excited about where we're going. Mountains to be climbed. Rivers to be crossed. Roads to be built. Friends to be found. Letters to be written. Songs to be sung.

There is more tomorrow. Laughter. Tears. New friends. Work to be done.

With too much clarity we see our failures and losses of yesterday. There was too much left undone — too much selfishness, too much stupidity, too much pride.

Now there is a place and time for a new beginning. The past is, in fact, past. This helps us plan for tomorrow. Make promises. Write resolutions. Start all over.

So I'm thankful for this place of stopping — and beginning again.

You Were Right, Lord

Like everyone else I've been caught up in the Christmas rush — the business, the excitement, the anticipation. All this Christmas season I've had little trouble thinking about the birth of Jesus.

That isn't always true. Usually I have to remind myself to keep Christ in Christmas.

I've been thinking a lot today about His birth. You know if I had been planning to save the world, I would have done it another way. I would have picked a young man. A healthy, intelligent, ambitious young man. About forty years old. Not a baby.

And I would have sent him to a large city, a center of power, a communication center, a place of political influence — not to a village named Bethlehem.

And, surely I would have sent him into a family of prestige and wealth — especially wealth. Rich people can do more than poor people. He should have had an important name. I wouldn't have sent him to a carpenter's home.

And, of course, I would have made him a white man, not a Jew. The Jews have been oppressed, despised, and mistreated for centuries. They didn't even have their own nation, and they are a minority group. No, I wouldn't have let him be born a Jew.

And I wouldn't have sent angels to shepherds. Maybe to priests or prophets. Maybe to governors and Caesars. But not to shepherds.

No, I wouldn't have done it the way God did it at all. But everything He did on that first Christmas makes sense to me — now. It was right, of course.

And I'm thankful for what He did and the way that He did it. I'm thankful for the Christmas story.

Our Fragile Unity

Pastors spend a lot of time trying to keep diverse people working together. It isn't easy! We don't often talk about it to other people. We don't often talk about it to God. But it's true! One of the major problems in church life is unity and cooperation.

I guess there are many reasons for church members to argue, become hostile, critical and fragment their interest. The history of the church is replete with stories of schism, division, and dissent. This is the story of Mark and Paul. The story of the Reformation. The story of nearly every local church.

As long as men are free to choose and as long as they have freedom of conscience, they are going to have diverse ideas. Some of this diversity is in their concepts of the Lord and His work. Some of them disagree about right and wrong. A lot of it is related to church government and the methods of church operation.

And, there are always people with mixed motives. In our generation there are men who are bossed around at work, who are dominated by strong women, and who try to exert their own personality in the church. These people cause trouble.

And, there are those who "use" the church. The church is their power house for appropriating prestige, praise, and ego. Others are able to make money off the church and the church members.

Even with these ulterior motives and often obvious purposes, the church usually tolerates the trouble makers. Not only tolerates, but sometimes capitulates to them.

I don't know, Lord, how churches hold together and have as much motivation and unity as they do have. Unless it is true that You do, in fact, love the church and direct the church, in spite of our fragile unity. So, I thank You for what we do have.

The Old Lady—The Smiling Child

The old lady hasn't been a member of our church too long. She was regular in attendance and made friends easily. Now she is bedfast and dying with cancer. I just came from her bedside.

Our people have been good to her. The ladies go in and clean her house. They prepare meals for her and her husband. They take her to the hospital for treatments and to the doctor for examination. Our people have helped her husband. They visit with them, pray with them and are being good friends. The old couple have no relatives near here and they have to depend upon the church people for help and for love. Church people often do this so well.

Anyway, today the old lady said, "Preacher, do you know who means the most to me in our church?"

I did not try to guess, so she told me.

"Mary Ann", she said.

I was perplexed. Mary Ann is a teen-age retarded child. Her body is distorted and crippled. She has the mind of a four year old — hardly a likely person to be valued by a dying old lady.

Understanding my perplexity, the old lady explained. Said that the first time she visited our church and every time she had come to the church building, Mary Ann was always by the front door. Mary Ann always greeted her, greeted her with a huge, warm smile. Mary Ann's smile and greeting made the old lady feel good. Made her happy. Made her glad.

Tonight I'm thinking about Mary Ann with her gift to smile. A smile that makes people feel better. And I'm thankful to You for that smile. And for the dying old lady who is thinking about a smiling child while she is dying.

A Long Wait

Maybe this all sounds sentimental and like a cheap novel, but it was refreshing to me and I'm glad I was a part of it.

Albert is a confirmed bachelor. He is just past his 68th birthday. Several years ago I baptized him and we have been friends since that time. He lives alone in a clean little house. He retired after years of service as a city fireman. He fishes, travels, collects stamps and reads paper back books.

As far as I know Albert never drank too much. Never dated much. He took care of his aging parents until they died. He did go to the races twice a year and bet the horses. He is shy. Quiet.

He came in this morning to tell me about Elaine. Seems that Albert and Elaine went through elementary school together. They became sweethearts and were going to marry. Everyone thought they would. A perfect match the people said. The parents approved. A wedding date had even been set.

Elaine went to an Aunts for two weeks to help with house work while the Aunt recuperated from an illness. During the two weeks Elaine got "into trouble". Albert looked at the floor when he told me.

Anyway, Elaine married the boy that was the father of the child. They were married for nearly fifty years. Elaine has grown grandchildren. She had a good life.

Her husband died last year. Albert waited for six months before he went to see Elaine. Said that he had always loved her — that he wanted to marry her. Today she agreed to the marriage.

I believe Albert. I believe that he was and is incapable of loving anyone but Elaine. I think that he has waited for this wedding for fifty years.

I'm glad to be in on this wedding.

On Marriage

One of the more important assignments given to a Pastor is performing marriage ceremonies. More often than not, at least in my case, I don't know the people who want to get married. They call me up or come by to see if I will marry them in the church building. I always set a time for a pre-marriage conference.

Marriage is under fire today. A lot of young people have given up on marriage, they just live together until they decide to give it up. They used to call it "trial" marriage, but they don't use that language now. About one-third of all marriages end up in divorce. This is a discouraging fact and an alarming statistic. Of course there is another large percentage of marriages that are dominated by conflict, fighting and hostility. Apparently about two thirds of all marriages are failures. This is discouraging, too. I guess it's not surprising that some young people give up on marriage.

But in spite of that dismal record of divorce and conflict, marriage is still desired by most young people. Many of them want to have a church wedding. It is one way that the church can and does still touch young lives at a crucial point.

I'm not as excited about weddings as I used to be. I've heard too many sad and tragic stories about unhappy marriages. I've spent too much time listening to husbands and wives fight. All of this conflict and divorce has made me more cautious about weddings. Not cynical, just cautious.

And then today I visited an elderly friend, John Harmon, in the hospital. He is dying, Mrs. Harmon, his beloved companion of fifty-four years, is sitting by his bed. They don't talk much. They don't have to. Their love and affection permeates the sick room and it has an eternal flavor. Death won't change it.

So it can work. A marriage can last and can be beautiful, even for fifty-four years. Thanks, Lord, for that reminder!

Sweet Songs

In our church tradition there has always been music. Apparently the first century Christians sang. A teacher of mine thinks that much of the New Testament is hymns. Music is a valid and authentic way for us to praise God and for us to express some of our deep feelings.

We have a wide variety of tastes and forms in music. Some religious music is solemn, some is joyful. Some is intricate, some simple. Some has rhythm and a beat, some is majestic. We use orchestras, organs, choirs, chorals, and ensembles. Now the rock groups are in church and the kids get turned on by religious rock.

Even with the various forms of music, there is still a kind of mystery about church music. I'm thinking tonight of some people that I know who sing in church. The mystery is not in their talent, or the beat, or the complexity of the music. It is not in the words. It is not in the sound. The mystery is in the singer.

I've watched and listened to people with enormous talent and skill who bomb-out on church music. They are inadequate with church music. Maybe they don't believe it. Maybe they don't feel it. Maybe they are too aware of being on stage. Maybe they wait for applause. I don't know, but there are just some people that can't effectively sing church music.

Then there are those people who do not really have much talent. Their skills and gifts are limited, yet they communicate. They sing to people. They seem to get it all together and touch something inside the listener. Every church seems to have this kind of person. I think there have always been people like this.

So, Lord, I thank You for people along the way who have sung to me — sweet singers of song. Sweet people who are able to speak what I feel in ways that I can never speak.

Geneva

I was thinking tonight about Geneva. It was late when I got home from one of the endless meetings that churches have. I finished some desk work, turned off the lights and made the familiar walk in darkness to the bedroom. This walk in darkness reminded me of the blind, who always walk in darkness. When I think of the blind I always think of Geneva.

She must be about forty now. She was a school teacher before a brain tumor and subsequent surgery left her blind. She is a Negro — a very large and attractive woman. She was engaged to be married when she lost her sight. She has no family in our city. An elderly couple live with her.

Geneva hasn't learned to read braille. She listens to the radio and yearns for company. Our church put a phone in for her and that gives her something to do. She uses the phone to keep up with her friends. Occasionally someone will read to her, but the radio and telephone keep her company most of the time.

My Mother and Geneva were telephone friends.

When Mother died they brought Geneva to the funeral home. She had never seen Mother, but they had built a good friendship through the telephone. They had understood each other. I guess they loved one another.

I heard a lady trying to tell Geneva what Mother looked like in death. And I saw tears come from Geneva's sightless eyes.

Somehow I knew a little better the fact of blindness.

Somehow I understood better that we do not need to see everything or to see anything to love and be loved.

I thank God for Geneva.

Joy

The other day a doctor told me that an old lady had just given up. She didn't want to live any longer. He said that she didn't enjoy life.

I've been thinking about that today. I enjoy life! Oh, there are a lot of things that I don't like. A lot of things that are unpleasant and disagreeable. A lot of people that rub me wrong. A lot of pain, hurt and frustration. A lot of sins and mistakes — my own and others.

I enjoy knowing that I'm here for a purpose. That my birth, my being, my very existence has some purpose. There is some reason for me being me. A feeling of purpose gives me identity and some self-value.

And I enjoy finishing an assigned task. I enjoy participating in a project that requires hard work. I enjoy tackling some difficult assignment. Too often I quit, give up, drop out. But I really enjoy sticking out an assignment.

I enjoy doing my duty. Even with all of the talk about "great gray areas" of behaviour, I still pretty well know what is right and what my duty is. There is joy and peace when we do the right thing. The right thing at home, with our friends, in the church or in society.

Guess the things I enjoy most are with other people. Not that private things like reading, writing, and praying aren't important. But I enjoy people more than I enjoy privacy. Real joy comes from helping someone, listening to someone, loving someone, speaking to someone, forgiving someone. Happiness and joy seem to be free gifts for those that care about other people.

There are a lot of things that I enjoy, Father. Thanks for helping me find some joy.

A Grump

A fellow told me today that I appeared to be happy and in good humor. You know people don't tell me things like that very often. Maybe it's because people don't usually comment to other people about their happiness. The real reason is probably that I don't often reveal happiness and good humor — and that's a shame.

I'm embarrassed to admit that, in spite of my undeserved and unexpected blessings, I'm too often cross, pre-occupied, ungrateful and dour.

My, my Lord! How much there is to be happy about!

The mockingbird singing this morning at dawn, and the ears to hear the song. The honey-suckle bush in the back yard breaking into fragrant bloom, and the ability to enjoy that fragrance. I stopped when I got the paper and watched the white clouds floating in a blue Kentucky summer sky.

A man should be happy when he eats breakfast with his two healthy, alert children. Who can be dour when the house is punctuated with a child's replay of last night's ball game and three straight hits? So what's wrong with today when you share it with your wife of nearly twenty years? You've shared a lot together.

And, I have a job that I like. I work with people that I enjoy. Yesterday I made a new friend and built an old friendship stronger. I read, wrote, drove, talked, walked, ate and slept. It was just fine.

Today is rich with promise. There are hours left. People to help and people who will help me. There is a laugh, a tear, and a feeling left in today. Miles to go before sleep.

I'm really sorry if I've been a grump. There is no reason for it, Father.

Thanksgiving

I'm thankful for my little girl, who isn't little anymore. It's hard for Daddys to understand that fourth grade girls aren't little. Not that they are grown. Maybe Daddys need "little" girls more than we realize. We need their love, their excitement, their chatter, their laughter, their play, and their incessant questions. I'm thankful for this particular time in her life and the joy, pure joy, she brings me.

I'm thankful for my boy, who is long past being little. Sixteen and six foot. Daddys need sons. We need their quiet friendship and respect. We need to know that someone watches us and occasionally imitates us. We need to watch them grow, learn and mature. I need my boy and I'm thankful for him.

I'm thankful for my wife. There is something secure and valuable about a twenty-year marriage. A twenty-year marriage doesn't have the romance and flowers of the first year and it doesn't have the sentiment and nostalgia of forty years. But it does have the durability and affection, the understanding and compromise, the mutual dependence that two decades together can bring. I'm thankful for my home.

I'm thankful for the memory of my parents. Since they have been gone those memories are indeed more cherished and precious. It's good that memory can fill lonely moments and enhance life. Memories are very real, and good memories have unspoken worth.

I'm thankful for the things I enjoy. A good breakfast. A good book. Shoes that fit. Country ham. Chocolate cake. Fresh corn. A baseball game. A bird song. An oak tree. A singing brook. Piano music. An evening with a dear friend. My pulpit. The Book of Ephesians. A newspaper. The right to vote. Someone who needs me. Dogwood in bloom. Money to spend and money to give. My church members. Children at play. A good sermon. Answered prayer. My blind friends. Free speech. My automobile. My secretaries. Gatlinburg. Other churches. John Sherman Cooper. A spring rain. Dedicated doctors. Eyesight. Jesus, Who visited this planet and Who made everything different. From deep within my heart I am thankful!

I Believe That I Have Helped

And now you have met the people. You have seen, heard and felt the way I feel about these people and the way I feel about my role in their lives. They are not uncommon people. They live on every street in America. They attend every church in America. They are legion. They are real and they are fiction. You know them even though you have never met them.

Over the years idealism about people is moderated by experience. Idealism, even religious idealism, just won't wash. We use a lot of catch words. Evangelism. Conversion. Born again. New creatures. Baptism of the Spirit. Repentance. Child of God. Getting saved. And, there are dramatic, profound, uncanny stories of personal change. Some people exhibit a kind of spectacular religious change. It happens often enough to keep us hopeful. It happens often enough to keep us excited.

But most of the time change happens subtly, if at all. There are two steps forward and at least one step back. There is the unwelcome fact of failure and hurt. All of us make a pilgrimage. A kind of slow, monotonous, journey through life. There are detours, distractions and pitiful interruptions.

I have been candid about my work. It seems that there has been more frustration, failure and tears than I expected. What have I really done for God and His people that has been successful? Has anything worked?

Well, I'm not sure how God keeps score.

Preachers, church members and denominations have their own system of keeping score. We like to count. We like to measure, weigh, graph, compute, and number. We like to build things, gather into barns and banks, and recite statistics. Not that numbers, buildings and bank accounts are irrelevant. Not that prestige, popularity, and denominational assignments are unimportant. Not that victory and success are ugly or blasphemous words. It's just that I'm not sure how God keeps score.

And I'm not really sure what I can expect of Lily Rose and all of the others. Where do I draw a line that circles Lily Rose out? When do I give up on these people? When do I leave them alone to work out their own salvation? Sometime I decided that my job was to stick with them. Slug it out. Tough it out. Be there. Cry. Listen. Laugh. Pick up. Share. Hang in there. Or, to be Biblical, be faithful and persevere. I believe that I have helped.

I am not cynical about Lily Rose or about my role in her life. It is satisfying. It is even fun to be

involved with people. There are no pat answers.
No magic formulas. No religious wands to wave.
We just walk hand in hand. We talk quietly. We
hurt together. We laugh when we can. When we
fall, we both have mud on our clothes. When we
fail, we both get an "F". We sing the same songs,
whisper the same prayers, worship the same God,
and seek refuge and hope in the same Saviour.

No way that I can make this trip alone. Sure, I
need and have the companionship of The Friend.
But He and I both feel more comfortable when
Lily Rose and all of the others join us along
The Way.

Occasionally all of us think about quitting. The
people, the frustrations, the pain, the loneliness
get to us. But who wants to cop out? It's too
interesting and the journey is too long to go it alone.